HEALING TODAY

HEALING TODAY

When the Blind See and the Lame Walk

MARK STIBBE and MARC A. DUPONT

Authentic

First published in 2005 by Authentic Media,
9 Holdom Avenue, Bletchley, Milton Keynes, MK1 1QR, UK
and
129 Mobilization Drive, Waynesboro, GA 30830-4575, USA.
Authentic Media is a division of Send the Light Ltd,
a company limited by guarantee (Registered Charity No. 270162)

British Library Cataloguing in Publication Data
A catalogue record for this book is available from the British Library

ISBN 1-86024-517-X

Cover design by fourninezero design.
Typeset by Waverley Typesetters
Print management by Adare Carwin
Printed and bound by J. H. Haynes & Co., Sparkford

CONTENTS

FOREWORD

BILL JOHNSON

We are blessed to have two gifted men join their efforts in bringing us a much-needed volume on the place of healing in the ministry of the Gospel of Jesus Christ today. This book wouldn't have been needed two thousand years ago. The church then believed all sickness was from the devil, and healing was from God. Today the attitude for most in the western world is the opposite – they sincerely believe that sickness is given (or at least allowed) by God to make us holy, while those who pursue healing are on the fringe at best, and from the devil at worst. It's amazing how far a cope can fall in two thousand years from such a clear God-given mandate. Marc A. Dupont and Mark Stibbe have done well to expose such a lie, and at the same time contribute something that is both profound and simple.

The ministry of healing is one of the most controversial aspects of the gospel today. Our unbelief makes it so. It is much easier to deny its place in ministry than it is to grapple with the unanswerable questions that arise as we cry out for this much-needed breakthrough. Thankfully, the authors did not back down from pursuing this expression of Jesus' ministry in their own lives, even when the walls of opposition and mystery seemed overwhelming. They have tasted for themselves that God is truly good.

Much like the late John Wimber, who had a gift for demystifying the mysterious, Mare and Mark have made this ministry both desirable and doable. Wimber had an ability to make people think that with God they could actually do the impossible. Since his home-going we have needed leaders to pick up this mantle and stir up the everyday believer to their privilege of participating in the miraculous. With clarity and precision, they make their case for this ministry to be taken outside of the four walls of the church. As a result, they are not giving us a book of theories. No, they have dug deep into their own experiences to bring us fresh insight into the record of scripture and the testimony of today's risk takers. While theories have their place, today's obvious need is for fathers – examples that we can follow. That is their gift to us.

BILL JOHNSON
Senior Pastor, Bethel Church, Redding, CA
and author of *When Heaven Invades Earth*
and *The Supernatural Power of a Transformed Mind*

Introduction

NOT ONLY WITH WORDS . . .

MARK STIBBE

Marc A. Dupont and I have a close friendship that has spanned some ten years. During that time, we have ministered together at many conferences; these have always involved healing prayer and nearly always teaching on divine healing. Marc has also been a good number of times to the church where I am the senior leader, St Andrew's Chorleywood, UK. Every time Marc has visited, the emphasis has been on evangelism and healing and we have seen people come to know Jesus Christ, while many have received divine healing both physically and emotionally. Together we have a combined experience of nearly forty years of ministering, both in a sustained way in the local church and on the road in itinerant ministry all over the world. We share many passions, but chief among them all is a passion to see the Kingdom of God extended through the preaching of the Gospel and through signs and wonders. It is this passion and experience that we want now to distil in book form in this volume, *Healing Today: When The Blind See and the Lame Walk*. The title is taken from the New Living Translation version of Matthew 11:4–6, where Jesus is talking to several of John the Baptist's disciples. John has been imprisoned by Herod and is awaiting execution. He is clearly experiencing considerable emotional agony as

he sits in the darkness of his dungeon, at the mercy of a
capricious king. In the midst of his turmoil he sends his
followers to Jesus to ask whether he really is the Messiah.
Jesus replies by telling them what has been happening
through his ministry, quoting from Isaiah 61 to highlight
the fact that he indeed is the Messiah:

> Jesus told them, 'Go back to John and tell him about what you have
> heard and seen – the blind see, the lame walk, the lepers are cured,
> the deaf hear, the dead are raised to life, and the Good News is being
> preached to the poor. And tell him: 'God blesses those who are not
> offended by me" (Mt. 11:4–6).

The emphasis in Jesus' reply is very much on two things:
his words and his works. He begins with his works: the
blind, the lame, the lepers and the deaf are all being
miraculously healed, and even the dead are being raised.
Jesus then talks about his words: he says that the Good
News is being preached to the poor. What is the Good
News? The news that God's long-awaited Kingdom has
come and that all can enter it, including the poor and the
prostitutes. God's rule has arrived on the earth in Jesus'
ministry. It is a kingdom in which sinners are forgiven,
the sick are healed and oppressed people are set free. It is
not just a kingdom of words. It is a kingdom in which the
power of God transforms lives. As the Apostle Paul was
later to say in 1 Corinthians 4:20:

> For the Kingdom of God is not just fancy talk; it is living by God's
> power.

God's Word and God's power

The word translated 'talk' in the verse above is the Greek
word *logos*. The word translated 'power' in the same verse
is *dunamis*. *Logos* refers to what is spoken, the proclamation

of the Good News. *Dunamis* refers to the demonstrations of God's power that attended and confirmed the preaching of the Gospel, namely miracles such as conversion, healing and deliverance. In Jesus' ministry the two were integrated in a potent ministry of proclamation and demonstration. The same was true in the ministry of the Apostle Paul. When Paul reminded the Thessalonians of his first visit to them, he wrote, using the same Greek words, 'When we brought you the Good News, it was not only with words but also with power' (1 Thess. 1:5). Once again we see here the dynamic marriage of word and power, *logos* and *dunamis*.

It is one of the sad facts of church history that these two things have often been separated. Some have stressed the Word. Others have stressed God's power. Some have emphasized that it is all about the Bible. Others have stressed that it is all about miracles.

The truth is that these two things were never meant to be separate in the church. They were fused together in the ministry of Jesus and the New Testament churches. They are supposed to be fused together today. Indeed, there are great dangers when they are not. Those who stress the Word alone can, at their worst, veer towards Pharisaism. They can become a people with a cerebral, bookish religion in which only those who interpret the Bible in a certain self-righteous way are truly born again. But those who stress God's power are equally vulnerable. At their worst they can veer towards Gnosticism, an equally dangerous heresy in which only those who are privy to secret revelation are truly born again. Separating *logos* and *dunamis* in our walk with God is truly dangerous. It should carry a health warning.

The opposite is, however, just as true. Combining God's Word and God's power is extraordinarily potent, both within the church and outside. Those who revere and know the Scriptures, and who also know and minister in the manifest power of God, are really the hope of the world. Marc and I agree that the church needs to have both these emphases if it is to be truly effective in our postmodern world. We need to have an emphasis on the Bible, on studying and preaching the Word. But we also need an emphasis on God's power, on ministering to one another and to the lost in the mighty, miracle-working power of God. It is not 'either or'; it is 'both and'!

God's purpose and his presence

Many evangelical churches today are going down one of two routes. Either they are becoming purpose-driven, focused on winning people to Christ through preaching the Gospel in a seeker-friendly way, or they are developing into God-chasers, praying for God's presence to become manifest among his people so that the lost line up at the church's doors, desperate to receive salvation. Marc and I see this polarization everywhere. We see some churches going down the purpose-driven route (which usually means 'seeker sensitivity') and others going down the presence-shaped route. Some pursue the crowd while others pursue the cloud.

Marc A. Dupont and I share a desire to see churches equipped not only to fulfil their purpose to make disciples but also to know God's empowering presence. I can say with complete integrity that my friend Marc both teaches and models this marriage of *logos* and *dunamis*, or 'purpose' and 'presence'. Recently Marc came to St Andrew's Chorleywood for a week of evening meetings, preaching the Gospel and ministering healing. During that time he opened up the Scriptures and preached the Good News of the Kingdom of God. It was Bible-based and Christ-centred.

At the same time, I can remember the extraordinary sense of God's manifest presence in our church during those meetings. By the last night the place was absolutely packed, with sick people everywhere, some lying on the floor at the front of the church. Tremendous things occurred, life-changing things. I remember my next-door neighbour, not a Christian, running from one end of the church to the front when Marc asked people to come forward if they wanted to give their lives to Christ. Her life has been utterly changed from that moment on and she is a very committed member of our church.

Another thing I remember was a Muslim man being brought to that same meeting. One of our church members had been at a supermarket that afternoon. He was at the checkout with a young Muslim man who was clearly in some pain. My friend asked him whether he wanted to come to a healing meeting that evening in his church and the man said yes. We prayed for him and his back pain went instantly. When I invited people later to share testimonies, this Muslim insisted on coming to the microphone and sharing that he was healed. I asked him what he thought of Christianity and he said he was overwhelmed by the love and the power of Jesus.

Another thing I remember vividly from that same meeting was the healing of a lady called Valerie King. Her testimony is included in a chapter I wrote in a book called *The Big Picture 2*. You can read the whole story there, but I will quote just part of Valerie's testimony here:

> On Wednesday evening (Marc's last service) I had a very strong feeling at 8pm that I must go to his final meeting. I got there late and someone kindly found me a seat, as the church was bursting at the seams. Within minutes Marc asked all the people with back problems to stand; I stood, having had a bad back since the age of 14 (not something that had come along with 'old age', as I am now 61!). Marc

encouraged us to go to the front of the church to be prayed for. In my heart, I thought I couldn't be healed, but I said to the Lord, 'If you need to give me more pain to be able to heal me, then please do it now.' He did.... Great pressure on the base of my spine and lots of movement inside. Someone was praying over me from the front and back; it was a lovely feeling and very spiritual. I went home and heard a loud 'click' in my spine, but I was still in some pain, as always. I went to bed and in the night I was woken by another loud 'click' and a muscle movement in my spine. In the morning I stepped out of bed normally, not slowly, stiffly and painfully as usual. ... I couldn't believe it. ... I still can't! It has improved daily, every day since. (I've had two operations in the last six years!)

What is so wonderful about this testimony is that Valerie started coming to our church because her daughter became a Christian through Alpha. Valerie not only heard the Gospel and received the forgiveness of sins, she was also miraculously healed of a disability that had afflicted her for nearly fifty years! She responded to God's Word and she experienced God's power. This is truly the way the Father wants us to minister today. All we are doing when we combine *logos* and *dunamis* is continuing the works of Jesus and fulfilling our calling as a local church. We are not embarking on some weird, fringe or eccentric form of Christianity. When we combine *logos* and *dunamis* in our beliefs and behaviour, we are really returning to normative New Testament Christianity – to Christianity as it was always supposed to be lived. As Jesus said to the Sadducees in Matthew 22:29:

> *Your problem is that you don't know the Scriptures, and you don't know the power of God.*

Clearly Jesus expects us to know both the Word of God and the power of God!

The ministry of divine healing

One of the primary manifestations of God's power is divine healing. John Wimber used this expression (as many others have) in preference to other terms that are commonly employed in this ministry. 'Miracle healing' is problematic because the Bible teaches that some signs, wonders and miracles are counterfeits inspired by the devil. The phrase 'faith healing' is equally fraught with danger because it places the emphasis on a person's faith rather than on God. 'Supernatural healing' is difficult because the word 'supernatural' can refer to demonic as well as divine inspiration. 'Psychic healing' is also out of the question because it involves the use of occult practices such as clairvoyance that are forbidden in Scripture (see Deuteronomy 18:9–13). We prefer John Wimber's phrase 'divine healing' because it points to the source of true healing, the God and Father of our Lord Jesus Christ.

Right at the beginning of this book I want to be clear about what we mean by that. One of the most helpful definitions has come from the writer Ronald Kydd, whose book on healing (*Healing Through the Centuries*) I will be quoting in Chapter 4, when we look at 'models of healing prayer'. Kydd defines divine healing as 'the restoration of health through the direct intervention of God'. Here the emphasis is on God working directly in the life of a sick person, bringing healing in spirit, soul and body. While we should never rule out the possibility that God might use human medicine to restore people to health, the focus in this book will be much more on God's direct intervention and involvement in the lives of the sick and the oppressed. As Kydd remarks, 'The products of such intervention are miracles.'

Kydd goes on to make a useful distinction between two kinds of 'divine healing'. When discussing 'divine healing' it is vital always to begin with the healing ministry of Jesus. Jesus ministered healing in both a narrow and a wide sense. In the narrow sense he brought healing to individuals, and these healings were physical, emotional and spiritual in nature. But Jesus also ministered healing in a much wider sense than this. As Kydd puts it, 'Implicit in his ministry is the concern to restore health not just to human bodies and minds but also to human relationships and to social structures.' In this book we will not be dealing primarily with the wider understanding of healing, though this will feature at a few points. We will be mainly concentrating on healing in the narrower sense. This is not because we want to pander to some form of western individualism but because we see the healing of individuals as Jesus' first concern in his earthly ministry. If it was a priority for the Master, then it should be a priority for the servants too.

Marc A. Dupont and I believe that Ronald Kydd is correct when he writes:

> It is clear to me that the restoration of health through the direct intervention of God has continued throughout the history of the church, and at no point has it been more widely seen than it is now.

Divine healing is on the increase in the church today, and this all over the world. Furthermore, Kydd points to evidence that preaching about Jesus the healer, and then ministering healing in Jesus' name, is now the most effective means of ministering to the lost. As Raymond Fung (until recently the secretary of evangelism at the World Council of Churches) has recently written, 'Quantitatively the number one means of evangelism today, of people coming to faith in Jesus Christ, is probably ... healing.' This is our experience as well. When we preach about the healing ministry of Jesus, faith is greatly increased and people are saved, healed and set free.

The blind see and the lame walk

The focus in this book is therefore on ministering not just in *logos* but also in *dunamis*, not just in word but also in power. One of the principal demonstrations of God's mighty power is divine healing, and this happens today, indeed is happening more today than during the whole of church history. Neither Marc nor I believe for a minute in the false doctrine of *cessationism*, the belief that the spiritual gifts (such as healing and miracles) ceased at the close of the apostolic era at the end of the first century. I have provided arguments against this wrong teaching in my book *Know Your Spiritual Gifts*, as has Ronald Kydd in a book entitled *Charismatic Gifts in the Early Church*. To put it succinctly, Marc and I believe that in Jesus' name the lame still walk and the blind still see!

The truth is, we have seen both happening in our ministries. I remember not long ago ministering in Finland with a team from St Andrew's Chorleywood. We conducted an afternoon workshop at a conference on the theme of Jesus the Healer. I taught on the way Jesus only ever did what he saw the Father doing and on the importance of listening to the Father and being directed by prophetic revelation in healing prayer. We then modelled that by waiting on the Lord for words of revelation. Immediately one of my team had an insight about a young man whose right foot had been broken but had not healed properly. To cut a long story short, a young man who was operating the sound system eventually came forward and said that he came from the Czech Republic. He used to be a long-distance runner but was now lame. He had broken his right foot, had been refused treatment in Finland, and had travelled home to his country for an operation, doing irreparable damage to his foot in the process. As a result of that, he had not run since (this was several years after) except once, when he had lasted only a few minutes and had then been on his back in agony for days. The metal bolts that had been inserted into his foot to keep it all together had caused him extraordinary pain when he tried to do again what he loved most – running.

This young man, called Peter, received prayer. As he did so, the pastor's wife came forward and asked him to forgive Finland for refusing him medical care. He freely forgave the Finnish people and continued to receive prayer. I remember experiencing an extraordinary surge of faith and getting the conference to proclaim the words of Isaiah 40:31 over him: 'You shall run and not grow weary.' That night Peter ran for twelve minutes without stopping and shared with the whole conference how he had been completely healed. A year later he wrote to us at St Andrew's to say that everyone, including the medics, was marvelling at what had happened. There was now no trace of the injury and Peter was running like the wind without any difficulties. Truly, the lame still walk when we pray for them in Jesus' name!

And the blind still see as well. Now, Marc and I are not naive. We know that people sometimes do not receive divine healing when we pray for them. There are no easy answers as to why this occurs and we both freely confess that in divine healing we tread a narrow path between miracle and mystery. Yet, at the same time, we do see miracles. Both of us have known blind eyes opened. When John Wimber first ministered in the UK it was at St Andrew's Chorleywood in May 1981. John taught about the Holy Spirit and then invited God's power to come. As he did so, God manifested his presence in the church building. Scores of people were touched by the power of God in a life-changing way. One lady, blind in one eye, had her sight in that eye completely restored. When I arrived as the new senior leader of St Andrew's in January 1997, her daughter was still worshipping at our church and told me the story from her own lips.

So God heals the sick today as we pray for them in the name of Jesus. That is the theme of this book. In the first part we will be 'Introducing Divine Healing', looking in a down-to-earth and user-friendly way at some of the theological issues that surround divine healing. This will provide a biblical foundation for Part Two, where we look practically at 'Ministering Divine Healing', on how to pray effectively for the sick. Hopefully by the end you will feel empowered to have a go yourself.

We do not pretend that this book answers all the questions surrounding divine healing, or is somehow a new word or even the last word on this subject. At the same time we have both felt called by the Father to write down what we have learnt on this subject over a good number of years. We have felt humbled in the process. I believe it was Sir Isaac Newton who, at the end of a life of great scientific discoveries, said that he had merely been like a small boy finding a few pebbles before the vast ocean of knowledge. Both Marc and I feel similarly small. The Father's love is vast as the ocean, as the great Welsh hymn of the 1904 revival proclaims. In this book we have merely gathered a few pebbles. We have shared from our very tiny sum of knowledge what we have discovered about the way in which divine healing functions as just one expression of the unfathomable love of God. But if it helps even one local church to develop a vibrant and effective ministry of divine healing, we will consider the effort infinitely worthwhile.

Part 1

INTRODUCING
DIVINE HEALING

Chapter 1

'I Am the Lord Who Heals'

MARC A. DUPONT

'Lazarus, come forth!' shouted Jesus, to the amusement, confusion and consternation of a crowd of mourners. Immediately scepticism and sorrow turned to absolute joy and amazement as a body emerged from the cave-like tomb. The body, which had been wrapped from head to toe, walked freely out of the cave of darkness and into the light of day. Lazarus, the brother of Mary and Martha who had died four days previously and whose body should have been stiff and stinking, was amazingly alive and healthy.

Although the Gospels only relate two other accounts of Jesus raising the dead, his entire ministry, indeed his entire life on earth, was continually punctuated with supernatural miracles, deeds and events. In fact, to try to separate the miraculous signs and wonders from the story of Jesus would be to deny a huge portion of what he did during his time on earth. There is no getting away from the fact that Jesus, the fully human, fully divine being, regularly performed incredible and supernatural acts of great power. And not only did he continually perform these great feats, but he trained and encouraged his disciples to do the same. According to the Gospel of Matthew, Jesus instructed the twelve disciples to 'heal the sick, raise the dead, cleanse the lepers, cast out demons' (Mt. 10:8).

There are those today who would argue that God only performed such miraculous healings through the early church and the twelve apostles as signs until the 'New Testament' portion of the Scriptures had been written and canonized. However, that argument does not stand scrutiny when the whole of the New Testament is examined. The Apostle Paul, whom God used to perform extraordinary miracles, instructed the church of Corinth to seek God for 'spiritual gifts' whereby they might move in supernatural healings and miracles themselves. The Apostle James stated that through prayer (at least by elders in a local congregation) the sick would be healed. God inspired these verses for the encouragement and instruction of the church throughout the ages, not just for one or two generations. But to really understand God's desire to heal the sick, diseased and afflicted one must take a fresh look at who, essentially, God is.

Jehovah Rapha

If we were to gather a dozen Christians with a basic knowledge of the Bible and ask everyone to list the top fifteen attributes of God, many of the lists would be quite similar. Most, if not all, of the participants would list attributes such as sovereign, merciful, gracious, creative, majestic, omniscient, omnipotent, holy, etc. All these attributes of God are certainly very close to the essence of God's being. The truth is, however, that while God has many, many wonderful and powerful attributes, there are just a few at the very core or centre of his being. And those core attributes shape and modify everything he has done and will do.

For example, we would be correct to say that God is completely sovereign. That is to say that God can do anything he wants, any time he wants. Yet it would also be incorrect to say he can do anything he wants, any time he wants, for the simple reason that his core attributes modify how he utilizes his other attributes, such as his sovereignty. For example, the major core attribute of God is love. God is love, according to 1 John 4:8, 16. What this means is that God will never exercise his sovereign will beyond the confines of love, grace and mercy. Of course, there are those who would ask what kind of loving God would doom some to hell merely because they reject him. The answer is that he is a loving God who refuses to insist that anyone spend eternity with him who truly doesn't want to! However, the main point we want to emphasize is that God is entirely motivated by love and grace in everything he does and desires to do, because that is his core being.

Exodus chapters 33 and 34 tell the remarkable story of Moses' meeting with the glory of God at the mountain of the Lord. We could define God's glory as being the very core, or essence, of who God is. In the same way that a husband or wife in a healthy marriage will only reveal all of themselves to that one special love of their life, so God only reveals his glory to those who seek him with all their hearts.

Moses had a conversation with God in Exodus 33 in which God encouraged Moses that he would be with him and would anoint him for the task of leading the Hebrew people into the Promised Land. Moses, however, wanted more than the power and provision of God: he wanted to know the very heartbeat of God. So he requested that God show him his glory. God's response was:

> You cannot see my face, for no man can see me and live (Ex. 33:20).

In other words, God said to Moses: you are not ready yet to fully gaze upon my core being, because I am holy, and sin cannot come that close to me. It would only be by the blood of the Lamb, Jesus of Nazareth, many centuries later that full payment would be made for the sins of humanity, restoring access to the glory of God.

Nonetheless, God could and often did reveal to certain individuals a foretaste or small sample of his glory. The holiness of God surrounds his throne, in much the same way that heat radiates well beyond the flames of a fire. According to Ezekiel 28:14 there are 'stones of fire' which act as a protective barrier to the very throne of God: not to protect God from us, but to protect us from the consuming fire of his holiness. But when we cry out to God and seek him with all our heart, we come into contact with revelation of the essence of who God is. And, just as God revealed a little of his glory to Moses in Exodus 34, we, too, find beyond the protective ring of fire more than we could ever hope or wish for. We find an all-powerful God consumed with unquenchable love for each of us.

When Moses ascended the hill of the Lord in Exodus 34, God had him stand on a rock and made a cleft, or cut, in that rock. As God's glory passed by, God covered Moses' face with his hand to prevent him from seeing that which he could only see much later with a glorified, or perfected, body. However, God did speak of his glory, or core being, as he passed by. He said of himself:

> *The LORD, the LORD God, compassionate and gracious, slow to anger, and abounding in loving kindness and faithfulness (Ex. 34:6).*

What many contemporary pulpits of anger and condemnation fail to grasp is that of the five defining traits of God's core identity, only one has to do with anger, and even there God said he was *slow* to anger! The very core heartbeat of God is compassion and grace, along with faithfulness.

The implications of this are enormous. What it means is that the eternal will of God is to shower humanity with kindness, favour, mercy and grace rather than anger, wrath and judgment. In other words, the will of God is to render towards each of us not so much what we deserve, but rather what we don't deserve: love.

The compassion demonstrated by Jesus

One of the primary ways God reveals his nature, or core identity, is through the names he gives himself throughout the Bible. For example, Deuteronomy 4:31 (NIV) says:

> *For the LORD your God is a merciful God; he will not abandon or destroy you or forget the covenant with your forefathers, which he confirmed to them by oath.*

In the first part of the verse God gives us one of his names, in the original Hebrew language. He calls himself *El Rachum* – 'the God of compassion'. We see this name which God uses of himself reflected time after time in the ministry of Jesus, the only begotten Son of God. For example, in Matthew 14:14 we read that Jesus healed many people because he felt 'compassion' for them. Mark 8:2 tells us Jesus fed a multitude of people out of compassion. Matthew 20:34 says Jesus was 'moved with compassion' to heal two blind men.

Compassion is more than merely feeling sorry for someone. Often when we see a street person as we are driving by, or see an advertisement in a magazine asking us to help starving third world children, we temporarily feel sympathy for that person or group. Rarely, however, does that fleeting emotion lead to an action that will have a significant impact in that person's life. Compassion is a touch or revelation of God's heart for that individual or group that compels you to actually *do something* that will be of real benefit to them. God's compassion is usually very specific with regard to who and when. It is, so to speak, God's rifle sight that zeroes in on someone in need. We are the bullets of love; he wants to send them. And often, as when Jesus directed the disciples to use their very limited supplies to feed a multitude, or to pray for someone with a deadly incurable disease, he is wanting to use us, in his love and provision, to accomplish something which would be impossible apart from his supernatural power and abilities.

I grew up for the most part in Southern California. San Diego, where we lived, is the homeless capital of the United States during the winter months because the weather is so agreeable. In the parks, on the beaches and in the tourist areas you can easily find homeless people begging for money, looking for handouts and scrounging in trash bins near grocery stores and restaurants. As I began to start in ministry in my early twenties, it was not uncommon to end up praying with street people and on occasion giving them money.

Years later I was on my first ministry trip in London. A friend who had joined me for the trip lived in Sweden. As we were walking back to our hotel after dinner one night, we passed a young man huddled in a cheap blanket in a shop doorway begging for money. My theology has always been to give as the Lord leads – as we are touched by God's compassion. As we walked by, I felt something burn in my heart for this young man – something far more than sympathy. I had ministered extensively in Mexico and to a lesser degree in Africa, where the poor and beggars are often present and you have to use discernment when giving money, because of the scam artists who can very effectively fake lameness. With this young man, however, I felt God directing me to reach out to him.

I told him I was a minister and asked where he was from and how he had ended up here, living on the streets of London, out in the cold. He told me that he had had a bad fight with his father in Scotland and had run away from home. I went on to ask him if he had ever known the love of Jesus. He explained that his family was a Christian family and he had often gone to church, but after repeatedly getting in trouble he had experienced a major falling out with his father. I then asked him whether, if he had the money, he would be willing to go home to his family and get right with his dad and the Lord Jesus. He began to cry and said that more than anything that's what he wanted to do. Although I had not been regularly involved in a street ministry, I had spent enough time with street people, runaways and beggars to have a bit of discernment concerning whether I was being scammed or not. When you first get into the world of street people it's a bit shocking to discover how many of the people on the streets are actually much better off than their appearance would suggest, at least in some first and second world nations. There are also a number of street people who have chosen to be on the streets simply because they refuse to work or take on any responsibility. This is not to deny that there are countless street people seriously in need of help and attention. Suffice it to say, however, that there are many con artists on the streets playing on people's emotions.

We gave the young man enough money to eat and to help get him a ticket home. He allowed us to pray for him, for safety and a real restoration with his dad. Afterwards, as we kept walking we passed many other street people looking for handouts. But with most of them we kept walking. What was the difference that compelled us to stop and minister to this young man and give him money? It was the compassion of God! It was the compassion of God, the Father, that compelled him to send his only begotten Son to live amongst, serve, and ultimately give his life for a humanity that had rejected his ways and love. It was the compassion of God that compelled Jesus to do the countless miracles and healings he did. It was the compassion of God that led Jesus to train, equip and encourage his disciples to do the things he did. And because God is the same yesterday, today and for ever (Heb. 13:8), he still desires to pour out his compassion on hurting, needy people. Jesus himself is seated at the right hand of God the Father, and that means that the present-day church, the body of Christ, is to be his present-day hands and arms reaching out to do wonderful and supernatural works of compassion. It is an easy temptation for the contemporary church to reduce the Gospel message to words alone.

As the Apostle John stated:

> *Let us not love with word or with tongue, but in deed and truth (1 Jn. 3:18).*

Words, as important as they are, are not enough in demonstrating the power of God's love.

Jehovah Rapha – the God who heals

Another key name of God found in the Scriptures is *Jehovah Rapha*. The Hebrew word *Jehovah* means God, and the word *rapha* means to repair, or to make fresh, or to heal as a physician would a sick patient. Deuteronomy 32:39 says:

> *See now that I, I am he, and there is no god besides me; it is I who put to death and give life. I have wounded and it is I who heal.*

God is so much into healing and other radical acts of compassion that we even see him in the Bible healing people who were enemies of Israel, his own people. For example, Naaman was one of the leading captains of the King of Aram, who was continually trying to bring ruination to Israel. Naaman was a valiant warrior, highly valued and respected by his king. Unfortunately, he was also a leper. Lepers in those times were often stoned when they came anywhere near non-lepers, who feared contracting the disease. Naaman heard, however, that in Israel there was the prophet Elisha, who ministered healing by the power of God. When he came to Elisha, the prophet instructed him to dip in the Jordan River seven times. After doing so, Naaman, the enemy of Israel, was completely healed.

Some seven hundred years later, Jesus rubbed this in the face of the Israelites of his home town. He said to them:

> There were many lepers in Israel in the time of Elisha the prophet; and none of them was cleansed, but only Naaman the Syrian (Lk. 4:27).

The people of Nazareth became so enraged with him that they tried to throw him off a cliff. The problem was that their hardness of heart prevented them from understanding God's (and Christ's) heart of compassion and mercy. To their mind, the blessings of God had to be earned through a lifestyle of perfectly adhering to the law and traditions. Jesus stated to one group of religious leaders:

> But go and learn what this means: 'I desire compassion, and not sacrifice,' for I did not come to call the righteous, but sinners (Mt. 9:13).

A few years ago, while ministering near Beira, Mozambique, I was greatly surprised by a miracle the Lord did. It was not so much the miracle itself that was so startling, but rather the person who received the healing. We were doing a pastors' conference during the day with outreaches at night. Our church building consisted of a simple wooden platform under a tree, maybe ten by fifteen feet. It was at the end of a dirt field surrounded on three sides by the mud huts of the village. There was a crowd of some 2,500 people present. In addition there were witches at the back of the crowd trying to curse us. The major disturbance, however, was a group of about twenty hecklers off to the side, leaning against the nearest mud huts. They were drunk, for the most part, and continually yelling and cursing us.

I had been preaching the Gospel for some thirty minutes with a translator and now began to give invitations to turn to Christ and to receive prayer for certain physical ailments. At one point I felt the Lord wanted to heal people with lame legs. As I said this through the translator, one of the drunken hecklers from the side pulled himself up and hobbled over to the platform on a home-made crutch. We found out later that years previously in the civil wars in Mozambique he had been with a few men when a landmine exploded. The soldier ahead of him had been killed, and he had lost the use of his leg as a result of it being filled with shrapnel.

Shortly after receiving prayer he began running and leaping around. He was brought up onto the platform to testify to his healing, but I found he was still exceedingly drunk. In his drunkenness, however, he was still leaping around the platform in joy and amazement. I was able after a while to relate to him that it was the Lord Jesus who had healed him, and asked if he would like to surrender his life to Jesus. He emphatically said 'Yes'. As I began to lead him in prayer, the Holy Spirit came upon him and almost instantly he was sober and ended up on his knees repenting of his sins. While I was very cognizant of the wonder of what God was doing, I was a bit incredulous that God was healing and saving this man who moments before had been cursing the preaching of the Gospel. To put the experience in a nutshell, it was a great lesson regarding the wonder of God's compassion.

The question that begs to be asked by the contemporary church is whether we desire to truly reflect the God of the Bible. The historical God whom we know as the Lord God Jehovah is a God abounding in love, grace and mercy. He is a God who cares so deeply for hurting, broken people that he gave his only begotten Son, Jesus, to die on a cross to set us free from the disease of sin. We must not allow the power of God's compassion, which is so central to the person of God, to be anything other than central in our expression of his love to the lost and hurting. Moreover, we dare not allow words alone to be the primary tool of extending God's Kingdom. As the Apostle Paul stated so succinctly:

> The kingdom of God does not consist in words but in power (1 Cor. 4:20).

As Jesus demonstrated time and time again, the Holy Spirit was upon him (and subsequently on us) so that 'the blind receive sight, the lame walk, those who have leprosy are cured, the deaf hear, the dead are raised, and the good news is preached to the poor' (Mt. 11:5, NIV).

Chapter 2

The Healing Ministry of Jesus

MARK STIBBE

In Chapter 1 we meditated on one of the most magnificent and faith-lifting names of God in the Old Testament: *Jehovah Rapha*: 'The Lord who heals' (Ex. 15:26). The word 'Jehovah' means 'always in a state of being' and can be translated as 'the Lord who is ...'. 'Jehovah' derives from the Hebrew word *havah*, which means 'to be' or 'to exist'. Perhaps the best translation of Jehovah is the word 'forever'. The word *rapha* comes from a Hebrew word meaning to mend by stitching. It means 'to restore, to heal, to make healthful'. Combine the two words together and you get 'The Lord who is forever the healer'. What a great revelation that is! God is always the Lord who heals people. This is his nature. This is who he is.

In Chapter 1 we also saw how this name is just one of many Jehovah names in the Old Testament. Other equally powerful titles are:

Jehovah Nissi	the Lord our Banner
Jehovah Raah	the Lord who is Shepherd
Jehovah Shammah	the Lord who is There
Jehovah Tsidkenu	the Lord who is Righteous
Jehovah Mekoddishkem	the Lord who Sanctifies
Jehovah Jireh	the Lord who Provides
Jehovah Shalom	the Lord who is Peace
Jehovah Sabaoth	the Lord of Hosts

The strange thing about these titles is this: no believer doubts that God is still our banner, our shepherd, our peace, our righteousness, and so forth. But some believers do have a problem with the idea that God is still our healer. Yet God is still the Lord who heals. He did not stop with the end of the Old Testament or with the death of the last of the apostles. The important word is the word 'is'. God *was* our healer, yes. Both in the Old and New Testaments, and indeed since those eras, God has healed people. God *will be* our healer, yes, when Jesus returns and death will be no more. But he also *is* our healer, right now, in the present tense.

Let me put it like this. Did God ever stop being our righteousness? Did he ever stop being our provider? Did he ever stop being our peace? No, of course not! In the same way, he has never stopped being our healer – in a *literal* sense. He is still *Jehovah Rapha*, Forever our Healer. This is who God is eternally within himself. God cannot stop being who he is. If you are in any doubt about this, look at Jesus.

Jesus the healer

Christians believe that Jesus of Nazareth is the ultimate revelation of who God is and what God is truly like. He is the image of the invisible God. He is the complete representation of God's being and nature. No one has revealed God as fully as Jesus has. No one will ever be needed again to show us any more of God. More than any other religious figure in history, Jesus Christ reveals who God is and what he is truly like. For true Christians, this is simply a non-negotiable fact. Other religions may give fragmentary glimpses of God's reality and character, but it is Jesus who gives the full picture. He alone discloses the ultimate revelation that God is the most caring, tender, loving, patient, holy, awesome and faithful Father. As has been said many times before, other world religions may be religions of truth, but Jesus Christ displays the truth of religion.

All of this means that Jesus Christ is much more than just a great teacher or an amazing prophet. Yes, he was acknowledged as an astonishing *teacher*, one who taught with true authority – an authority direct from God, not derived from tradition. Yes, Jesus was acknowledged as a *prophet*. He was addressed as both in his own lifetime by many people. But Jesus is far more than either of these things. In his own ministry he gave more than a few hints that he was actually the human face of God.

One of the most compelling evidences for this is the way Jesus used the two simple words 'I am'. Sometimes he used these words without predicate (i.e. on their own, without qualification). So, in John 8:28, Jesus says:

> When you have lifted up the Son of Man on the cross, then you will realize **that I am he** and that I do nothing on my own, but I speak what the Father taught me.

At other times Jesus uses 'I am' with a predicate, with a qualifying statement:

> 'I am the bread of life' (Jn. 6:35)
> 'I am the light of the world' (Jn. 8:12)
> 'I am the gate' (Jn. 10:7)
> 'I am the good shepherd' (Jn. 10:11)
> 'I am the resurrection and the life' (Jn. 11:25)
> 'I am the way, the truth, and the life' (Jn. 14:6)
> 'I am the true vine' (Jn. 15:1)

The two words 'I am' may seem slightly strange to our modern ears, but to Jesus' own Jewish contemporaries they were full of significance. From a Hebraic perspective, 'I am' would have been understood as the divine name. In Exodus 3:14, God reveals himself to Moses with these words, 'I AM THE ONE WHO ALWAYS IS'. God discloses himself in Isaiah 41:4 in these words: 'It is I, the LORD, the First and the Last. I alone am he.' In using the two words 'I am', either on their own (as in John 8:28) or with a predicate, Jesus was obviously making a very powerful claim in terms of his self-understanding. He was saying effectively that he was Jehovah in human flesh. He was the 'I am' incarnate. What every reader has to decide is what Jesus' own contemporaries had to decide. Was Jesus demented, demonized or divine? He was accused, without grounds, of being demented and demonized. Christians believe he was and is divine.

What is the significance of all this for healing? One of the things a reader of the New Testament cannot fail to spot is that Jesus performed healing miracles. This is one of the most unmistakable features of Jesus' ministry. When Peter, the Galilean fisherman-turned-apostle, stood up on the Day of Pentecost, he described many things concerning Jesus. He covered the following subjects in one sermon (his *first* sermon):

1. The Human Jesus: 'Jesus of Nazareth was a man' (Acts 2:22, NIV)

2. The Charismatic Jesus: 'accredited by God to you by miracles, wonders and signs' (Acts 2:22, NIV)

3. The Crucified Jesus: 'You, with the help of wicked men, put him to death by nailing him to the cross' (Acts 2:23, NIV)

4. The Risen Jesus: 'God has raised this Jesus to life, and we are all witnesses of the fact' (Acts 2:32, NIV)

5. The Ascended Jesus: 'Exalted to the right hand of God' (Acts 2:33, NIV)

6. The Gift-Giving Jesus: 'He has received from the Father the promised Holy Spirit and has poured out what you now see and hear' (Acts 2:33, NIV)

7. The Divine Jesus: 'Therefore let all Israel be assured of this: God has made this Jesus, whom you crucified, both Lord and Christ' (Acts 2:36, NIV)

A comprehensive understanding of Jesus needs to embrace all of these aspects of his nature and acts. But for our purposes the important thing to remember is that Peter – who spent three years with Jesus – stresses that Jesus was a wonder-worker. Peter emphasizes that Jesus went about doing miracles. He starts off his celebration of Jesus with these words:

Men of Israel, listen to this: Jesus of Nazareth was a man accredited by God to you by miracles, wonders and signs, which God did among you through him, as you yourselves know.

Here Peter uses three words to describe Jesus' super-natural ministry: miracles, wonders and signs. He attributes these to a divine source by saying 'God did these'. He points out that these charismatic events were God's accreditation of Jesus. And he concludes by saying that all the Jewish pilgrims listening to Peter's message were well aware that Jesus had performed many divinely inspired miracles. He says, 'as you yourselves know'. And no one rose up in either Peter's time or after to contradict this fact!

Later on in the Book of Acts, Peter preaches another message about Jesus, this time not to a Jewish audience as in Acts 2:22 ('men of Israel') but to a Gentile one (Cornelius and his household). Here again Peter begins with the facts about the historical Jesus. He says:

> *I'm sure you have heard about the Good News for the people of Israel – that there is peace with God through Jesus Christ, who is Lord of all. You know what happened all through Judea, beginning in Galilee after John the Baptist began preaching. And no doubt you know that God anointed Jesus of Nazareth with the Holy Spirit and with power. Then Jesus went around doing good and healing all who were oppressed by the Devil, for God was with him (Acts 10:36–38)*

These words are very revealing. They show once again that Jesus was anointed with the power of God's Spirit and that this power enabled him to heal the sick. Here again we see Jesus the healer.

The certainty of Jesus' healing miracles

No serious scholar now doubts that Jesus healed the sick during his two- to three-year ministry. Eminent scholar Marcus Borg writes, 'On historical grounds it is virtually indisputable that Jesus was a healer and an exorcist.' There are many reasons why mainstream scholars (both Christian and non-Christian) agree with this conclusion. One is because there is what is called 'multiple attestation'. This is a technical way of saying that all the earliest sources concerning Jesus bear witness to the fact that he healed the sick. With so many different sources confirming the same thing, it is harder to believe that Jesus did *not* perform miracles than that he did. Another reason is that even Jesus' opponents did not challenge his powers of healing. No one at the time of Jesus denied that he healed the sick and delivered people from demonic oppression. The Pharisees questioned the source of Jesus' healing power (see Matthew 12:22–29), but they did not question the fact that he healed people.

So even sceptical scholars now admit there is commanding evidence for the healing miracles of Jesus. The old view of liberal scholar Rudolf Bultmann is now by and large discredited; he disdainfully and somewhat arrogantly wrote:

> It is impossible to use electric light and the wireless and to avail ourselves of modern medical discoveries, and at the same time to believe in the New Testament world of demons and spirits.

This view is now accepted by many as based on a naturalistic worldview rather than on objective, rigorous scholarship. Naturalism delights in explaining phenomena without reference to any supernatural causality. However, many people today recognize that the world cannot be explained without at least some reference to transcendent categories. Miracles are accordingly back in fashion.

A leading scholar in the field of Jesus' miracles is Professor Graham Twelftree. He writes:

> However reluctantly, the vast majority of students of the historical Jesus affirm that Jesus performed mighty works.

He goes on to add:

> The single most time-consuming aspect of Jesus' pre-Easter public mission was the performing of miracles.

He concludes:

> Any critical reconstruction of the historical Jesus must not only include but also, indeed, emphasize that he was a most powerful and prolific wonder worker.

Another leading scholar, Professor Gregory Boyd, agrees with Graham Twelftree's thesis:

> The amount of miracles he performed, the way he performed them, and the reasons he performed them, were all radically unique. Jesus is, plain and simple, one of a kind.

That last comment is very significant. Jesus, in the area of healing miracles, is 'one of a kind'. Jesus is quite simply unique. Yes, we have stories of other Jewish holy men (like the wonderfully named Honi the Circle Drawer) praying for miracles. But they are few and far between and the miracles tend to be answers to intercessory prayers rather than the result of direct commands. Gerd Theissen's assessment is therefore accurate:

> Nowhere else do we have traditions of so many miracles by a single miracle-worker.

Jesus stands alone and above all other charismatic figures of his age in this regard. The consensus view among reputable, mainstream scholars is that Jesus performed miracles of healing.

To summarize: Jesus performed more miracles than any other figure in the ancient world. More than that, Jesus' miracles have a far greater historical credibility and they are also far more impressive in terms of evoking awe and wonder. The miracles of Jesus are part of what scholars call the *ipsissima facta* or 'actual facts' about Jesus. To use scholar Birger Gerhardsson's categories, these miracles are either therapeutic (i.e. healing wonders) or non-therapeutic (i.e. miracles such as turning water into wine, walking on water, multiplying bread, etc.). In Mark's Gospel alone there are twenty miracle stories. If you add the summaries of healing events, this accounts for about one-third of the Gospel. Nearly 50 per cent of the first ten chapters of Mark's Gospel describe miracles, many of them therapeutic or healing miracles. That is a huge number by any standards. We cannot therefore avoid the conclusion that the historical Jesus performed extraordinary wonders – healing the sick, delivering the demonized, multiplying food, calming storms, and even raising the dead.

The source of Jesus' healing miracles

How did Jesus do these things? Over the last two thousand years there have been many suggestions, some of them extremely fanciful. Perhaps the most ludicrous of all was reported in a press article on Monday 6 January 2003, entitled 'Jesus healed using cannabis'! The reporter, Duncan Campbell, wrote:

> Jesus was almost certainly a cannabis user and an early proponent of the medicinal properties of the drug, according to a study of scriptural texts published this month. The study suggests that Jesus and his disciples used the drug to carry out miraculous healings. The anointing oil used by Jesus and his disciples contained an ingredient called *kaneh-bosem* which has since been identified as cannabis extract, according to an article by Chris Bennett in the drugs magazine, *High Times*, entitled 'Was Jesus a Stoner?' The incense used by Jesus in ceremonies also contained a cannabis extract, suggests Mr Bennett, who quotes scholars to back his claims. 'There can be little doubt about a role for cannabis in Judaic religion,' Carl Ruck, professor of classical mythology at Boston University, said. Referring to the existence of cannabis in anointing oils used in ceremonies, he added: 'Obviously the easy availability and long-established tradition of cannabis in early Judaism would inevitably have included it in the [Christian] mixtures.' Mr Bennett suggests those anointed with the oils used by Jesus

were 'literally drenched in this potent mixture. Although most modern people choose to smoke or eat pot, when its active ingredients are transferred into an oil-based carrier, it can also be absorbed through the skin'. Quoting the New Testament, Mr Bennett argues that Jesus anointed his disciples with the oil and encouraged them to do the same with other followers. This could have been responsible for healing eye and skin diseases referred to in the Gospels.

This is nonsense! Jesus did not heal the sick because there was cannabis in the oil he used; he healed the sick through the power of God's Holy Spirit. This is plainly evident when we look at Jesus' exorcisms. In Matthew 12:28 Jesus says:

> *But if I am casting out demons by the Spirit of God, then the Kingdom of God has arrived among you.*

These words make it abundantly clear that Jesus' healing and deliverance miracles were demonstrations of the Kingdom of God and performed 'by the Spirit of God'. In other words, within the self-consciousness of Jesus there was the recognition that his healing miracles were the result of him being empowered in a special – indeed supernatural – way by the Holy Spirit. This is surely why in Luke 4:18–19 he applies the words of Isaiah 61 to his life and ministry:

> *The Spirit of the Lord is upon me, for he has appointed me to preach Good News to the poor. He has sent me to proclaim that captives will be released, that the blind will see, that the downtrodden will be freed from their oppressors, and that the time of the Lord's favour has come.*

In Jesus' life, the sense of the plenitude of the Spirit's power was so strong that he knew with certainty that the end-time promises of God (such as Isaiah 61) were being fulfilled in his ministry.

All the liberating activities of his ministry, including healing, were therefore the result of the Spirit's anointing, not drugs or magic. As Professor James Dunn has said, 'His awareness of being uniquely possessed and used by the divine Spirit was the mainspring of his mission and the key to his effectiveness.' In other words, the Holy Spirit worked within and through him to effect healing miracles. The source of his healing miracles was neither medicine nor magic but the miraculous power of God's Spirit. The quest for the historical Jesus is in reality the quest for the Charismatic Jesus.

The character of Jesus' healing miracles

We should not envisage Jesus as using this power without love. In one of the earliest healing miracles in the Gospel, we read:

> *A man with leprosy came and knelt in front of Jesus, begging to be healed. 'If you want to, you can make me well again,' he said. Moved with pity, Jesus touched him. 'I want to,' he said. 'Be healed!' Instantly the leprosy disappeared – the man was healed (Mk. 1: 40–42).*

Here a key phrase is 'moved with pity'. The verb in the original Greek text is *splagchnizomai*. The first part of that verb, *splagchna*, literally refers to the bowels or the 'guts'. Loosely translated, this means that Jesus felt overwhelming compassion for the leper in the deepest parts of his being. When Jesus prayed for the leper's healing, he was moved viscerally, not just emotionally. He literally yearned for the man's well-being.

This word *splagchnizomai* is used twelve times in the Gospels, and always of or by Jesus. Matthew in his Gospel uses the word five times. So, for example, we read in Matthew 14:14 that 'a vast crowd was there as he stepped from the boat, and he had compassion on them and healed their sick'. Mark uses it four times and, as we have noted above, it is seen as the major motivating factor in his healing ministry. Luke uses it three times, including in Luke 7:13, when Jesus sees the widow of Nain (whose son he raises from the dead). As Luke reports, 'When the Lord saw her, his heart overflowed with compassion. "Don't cry!" he said.'

When we look at the miracles of Jesus, we see that there are essentially four kinds: miracles of healing, deliverance, nature and resurrection. All four kinds of miracle are attributed to the heartfelt compassion of Jesus in the Gospels. So we read of two blind men:

Jesus felt sorry for them and touched their eyes. Instantly they could see! Then they followed him (Mt. 20:34).

We read of the hungry crowds in Matthew 15:32, who are about to be fed through a miracle of multiplication:

Then Jesus called his disciples to him and said, 'I feel sorry for these people. They have been here with me for three days, and they have nothing left to eat. I don't want to send them away hungry, or they will faint along the road.'

In the case of the demon-possessed boy in Mark 9:22, the father appeals to Jesus' compassion in securing his son's deliverance by saying:

The evil spirit often makes him fall into the fire or into water, trying to kill him. Have mercy on us and help us. Do something if you can.

And, as we saw above, Jesus had great compassion on the widow of Nain before raising her son from the dead.

In every kind of miracle, compassion is the primary emotion felt by Jesus prior to and during the event. Jesus had compassion on those who were sick. Compassion – empathetic identification – was his first response to the ocean of human needs he confronted.

This was shown most graphically when Jesus put the needs of a sick person before law-keeping. Jesus came to demonstrate not the love of law but the law of love. For that reason, a number of his healing miracles were performed on the Sabbath. Compassionate love for people in great need transcended the drive to observe religious rules and regulations. God's love was the wellspring of his words and deeds, and no appeal to legal codes was going to stop him bringing freedom to desperate people. Jesus used God's power lovingly. His miracles reveal the God who is gracious and compassionate.

The purpose of Jesus' healing miracles

The healing miracles of Jesus cannot be separated from his teaching on 'the Kingdom of God'. The Kingdom of God is the rule of God on the earth. Jesus inaugurated an invasion of God's reign. This had been expected to come at the end of history and bring an end to the devil's hold on the cosmos. But in Jesus this invasion occurs ahead of time. The future breaks into the present.

So much has been written on this subject that my comments here will be few. Along with many other Bible scholars, I believe that one of the primary reasons why Jesus healed the sick was to demonstrate the presence of the Kingdom or rule of God. Jesus' ministry involved both proclamation and demonstration. From the start he preached that the Kingdom of God was very near. Not only did he proclaim it, he also demonstrated it, by healing the sick and delivering the oppressed. Sickness, sin, demonization and death represent the signs of the enemy's kingdom, the kingdom of God's adversary, Satan. When Jesus started to minister in Galilee nearly two thousand years ago, he defeated these signs of the kingdom of darkness wherever he went. As he preached and prayed for people, God's kingly rule advanced through his words and his works, pushing back the frontiers of Satan's rule. The healing miracles of Jesus are accordingly a demonstration that the long-awaited Kingdom of God has arrived now. Their purpose is intimately connected to revelation. They disclose the reign of God.

Having said that, we should note that Jesus also taught that the Kingdom of God was yet to come. Yes, on the one hand, he proclaimed and demonstrated that the Kingdom was already present. He pointed to his deliverance miracles as evidence of that (Mt. 12:28). On the other hand, he also taught his disciples to pray, 'your Kingdom come'. In other words, he commanded them to expect and pray for the fullness of God's Kingdom on the earth at a future date, the date of his return on the clouds in great glory (the Second Coming). This means – as many have argued – that the Kingdom is both *now* and *not yet*. It is here in part, but not yet fully here.

It is this insight that led German theologian Oscar Cullmann to propose an analogy for the time between the first and second advents of Christ. He likened this time-frame in which we now live to the one between D-Day and VE Day during World War II. D-Day in June 1944 signalled the beginning of the end for the German forces in Europe. The dark and oppressive domination of continental European nations by the Nazis had caused tremendous suffering. But the landings of the Allies in

Normandy initiated the final defeat of Hitler. From then on, victory in Europe was inevitable. It was only a matter of time before the end came and Europe could be liberated completely. However, even though victory was certain, between D-Day and VE Day the fighting was more intense and the casualties were more numerous than at any other time in the war. There is no enemy more dangerous than a cornered and defeated enemy.

The time-frame between the first and second advents of Jesus is like that between D-Day and VE Day. The analogy is not perfect, simply because no analogy is perfect. But it has helped many to cope with 'the paradox of miracle and mystery', as I call it. On the one hand we see many victories as we pray for the sick and for the oppressed. We see miracles. On the other hand, we live with many prayers unanswered; wonderful believers die young in spite of the most fervent and prolonged prayers. We see mystery. How are we to explain this? Is it that we have inadequate faith as we pray for them? Is it that they have insufficient faith as they receive prayer? Or is there a deeper reason, to do with the battle of the kingdoms?

Here again we must – in my view – constantly link healing miracles with the Kingdom of God. The Kingdom of God is God's future reign on the earth. It is life as it was always meant to be – without suffering, without illness, without hospitals and without cemeteries. When healing miracles happen, it is because the future rule of God has broken into history. When they do *not* happen, it is because this future reign of God will only be fully consummated at Christ's return. As Derek Morphew puts it very eloquently in his book *Breakthrough*:

> We can say categorically that healing occurs because the kingdom of God breaks through. We can say equally

categorically that healing does not occur because the kingdom of God has not broken through finally. No one can say what determines how frequently and on what basis this intervention of the powers of the age to come takes place. This is the mystery of the kingdom.

The purpose of the healing miracles of Jesus – both in his own ministry and today – has to do with demonstration. They demonstrate that the rule of God has broken into history ahead of time, as it were. When healing miracles do not happen, it is because this future rule has not been fully realized on the earth. The enemy is defeated but he fights viciously, holding on to what power he has until his certain end. While we celebrate every sick person healed in the name of Jesus, we should also in a paradoxical way celebrate the death of every faithful believer who dies of illness. In a very real sense such believers are casualties of war – a war between two kingdoms. As such, they should be given a soldier's burial. They should be given a hero's send-off. They have died, yes, but they will be raised on the last day when Christ returns and God's reign on the earth is completely established. They have suffered, yes, but they have suffered on the winning side. And one day they will be given the ultimate healing of bodily resurrection, and they will live in a city without a cemetery.

The context of Jesus' healing miracles

And yet it would be wrong to leave it at that. To be sure, all healing miracles are signs of the in-breaking rule of God. In that sense they are the work of the sovereign King of Kings. When healing happens it is because God the King has taken the initiative to manifest his rule. At the same time, healing miracles require some level of human co-operation if they are to occur. In other words, they require our faith. Faith is the context for healing.

This means that we cannot merely stress the Kingdom of God and leave faith out of the equation. The manifestation of the Kingdom is the God-ward side of a healing event. It is God's sovereign work. But for healing to occur, there needs to be faith operative somewhere – whether this is in the person receiving or in the people ministering. This is the human-ward side of the equation. Where there is no faith, there is no healing. Where there is some faith, there is some healing. Where there is a lot of faith, there is a lot of healing.

Jesus made it clear that faith was required if we are to experience the reign of God in our lives. In Mark 1:15 he proclaimed that people must repent and *believe* because the Kingdom is imminent. Believing is therefore a key entrance requirement to the Kingdom. Anyone who wants to see the reign of God manifested must have faith. This applies to miracles, which are visible manifestations of God's rule. So faith is important too. Indeed, the noun *pistis* (meaning 'faith') occurs five times in Mark's Gospel. What is significant is that all five occurrences are connected with miracles, including healing miracles:

Mark 2:5	(the healing of the paralytic)
Mark 4:40	(the stilling of the storm)
Mark 5:34	(the woman with the bleeding)
Mark 10:52	(blind Bartimaeus)
Mark 11:23–24	(the cursing of the fig tree)

Faith is the simple, childlike trust in God's power to save, heal and deliver when we pray in the name of Jesus. It seems that in most cases, faith is absolutely essential. Thus we read in Matthew 9:28 of Jesus' question to two blind men, determining whether they have faith for their healing:

They went right into the house where he was staying, and Jesus asked them, 'Do you believe I can make you see?' 'Yes, Lord,' they told him, 'we do.'

Here Jesus heals the blind men because the context is conducive to healing. In other words, there is faith in the house. Conversely, when there is lack of faith, the context seems not to be conducive to healing. So we see in Mark 6:5 that Jesus was inhibited from performing miracles of healing in his own town because of unbelief:

And because of their unbelief, he couldn't do any mighty miracles among them except to place his hands on a few sick people and heal them.

All this means that we must be very careful not to over-simplify healing miracles. Sometimes healing miracles happen today when we pray in the name of Jesus. Sometimes they do not. Any formula that chooses to live on the extreme end of a theological polarity is doomed to eventual disappointments. Those who overemphasize the Kingdom view of healing can end up with a passivity that says, 'It's all up to God.' Those who overemphasize the faith view of healing can end up with an activism that says, 'It's all up to me.' The truth is, healing miracles are a dynamic, mysterious cooperation between God's sovereign will (Kingdom) and our desperate believing (faith). It is not 'either or' but – as in so many things – 'both and'.

The continuation of Jesus' healing miracles

Let's return to where we began, with the wonderful revelation of God as 'the Lord who heals' (Ex. 15:26). God has not stopped being the Lord who heals any more than he has stopped being the Lord our provider. As God says in Malachi 3:6 (NIV), 'I the Lord do not change.'

Furthermore, Jesus Christ came into the world to reveal God's nature. He too used the name 'I am'. He demonstrated that he was the God who heals both in his message and in his miracles. Jesus reflected this aspect of God's unchanging nature in his earthly ministry. He continues to reflect this aspect of God's unchanging nature today. Thus we read in Hebrews 13:8, 'Jesus Christ is the same yesterday, today, and for ever.'

In my book *Prophetic Evangelism* I told the story of how the Lord had spoken to me one evening that the next day he was going to heal people of ME. This was while I was doing the morning Bible readings in the main tent at New Wine summer camp in 2003. The following morning he indeed did heal people of this condition. In 2004, I was back at New Wine doing seminars on prophetic evangelism. It was an absolute joy for me to have one lady stand up and testify to how God had miraculously healed her the previous year of ME – a condition that had completely destroyed her life for over fifteen years. She stood in front of the hundreds of people that morning to tell everyone what Jesus had done for her that morning in 2003, how she was now working full-time, and how her whole life had been restored. Then she went back to the kitchens to continue a thirteen-hour stint serving others. Truly Jesus Christ heals the sick today!

Jesus has not ceased his healing ministry; he continues it, in and through his body, the church. Every day, literally thousands of people all around the world are receiving healing as they are prayed for in Jesus' name. Even as you read this right now, someone somewhere in the world is receiving a healing miracle. Someone somewhere is experiencing the Kingdom of God – God's presence in strength.

I believe there will be more and more healing miracles the nearer we get to the return of Jesus Christ on the last day. Jesus said in Matthew 13:31–32:

> *The Kingdom of Heaven is like a mustard seed planted in a field. It is the smallest of all seeds, but it becomes the largest of garden plants and grows into a tree where birds can come and find shelter in its branches.*

Underline the word 'grows'. The rule of God is an ever-increasing, ever-expanding divine reality on the earth. It is not static. It is dynamic. If the Kingdom of God is to go on advancing throughout the earth, and if healing miracles are visible demonstrations of God's rule, how could they cease? How could they not increase?

In 1997 I published a book (still in print) called *Know Your Spiritual Gifts*. I would like to finish this chapter by quoting something I said there about miracles, especially miracles of healing. I have not changed my view at all since writing these words. If anything, they carry more conviction today than when I first wrote them:

> For me the great beauty of miracles lies in their relationship to the Kingdom of God. The Kingdom of God has been inaugurated in Jesus' first coming and will be consummated in his second. Miracles are signs of the Kingdom; they are outward signs of the invisible, dynamic rule of God. When Christ returns on the last day, the promise of Scripture is that God will create new heavens and a new earth out of the fabric of the existing heavens and earth. He will perform the miracle of immediate, cosmic recreation. In the meantime,

every person who witnesses a miracle in the name of Jesus is witnessing a 'trailer' of the eschatological re-creation of the world. Every time a dead person is raised to life, we catch a glimpse of the unimaginable miracle of the final resurrection of the dead at the *parousia*. Every time a person is miraculously healed, we are given a foretaste of the wholeness which will be ours as we feed from the leaves of the tree of heaven. Every time God intervenes in nature to multiply loaves or to calm storms, we are given a hint of 'Paradise Regained' – nature once again under the sovereign rule of God. The great beauty of the gift of miraculous works is that it affords us a momentary 'apocalypse' or 'unveiling' of tomorrow's world. As such, the nearer we get to God's tomorrow, the more we can expect to see miracles occur. So, Lord, let the miracles happen in our midst! Let your Kingdom come, and let there be signs and wonders throughout the world.

Chapter 3

Fearfully and
Wonderfully Made

MARC A. DUPONT

What is man that You take thought of him,
And the son of man that You care for him?
Yet You have made him a little lower than God,
And You crown him with glory and majesty!

Psalm 8:4–5

The Gospel story is the ultimate story of romance. It is the definitive story of a Prince Charming wooing an ugly bride-to-be, who at first has no desire for him. What could compel Jesus to give up his life so selflessly for humanity, which was now all but rejecting him? What could compel God, the Father, to give up his only begotten Son and send him to earth to be rejected, tortured and crucified by the very humanity he had created? Just one thing: his great love for us. The love and compassion of God, as we discussed in the first chapter, is the foundation for all the healing and blessings God longs to bring to our lives. But in order to establish a sustaining faith and understanding of the love of God for each of us, we need to understand exactly what, or more precisely who, we are in his eyes.

The value of one

Jesus told a parable concerning a shepherd with a flock of one hundred sheep who lost one of them. In the story, the shepherd left the ninety-nine behind to look for the lost one. Jesus compares this with God's love for each of us. The shepherd's actions, like the Gospel, are so contrary to the natural thinking of most of us. We would think, 'Well, we've lost one, but let's put it into perspective – we still have ninety-nine, so let's rejoice over what we've got and make sure we don't lose any more. Let's not go to too much trouble here – after all, we're still well off.' Jesus continued the story by saying:

> *And when he comes home, he calls together his friends and his neighbours, saying to them, 'Rejoice with me, for I have found my sheep which was lost!' (Lk. 15:6).*

Clearly this shepherd had a different perspective on the worth of that one lost, troublesome sheep to that which most of us would have. Jesus completed the parable by saying:

> *I tell you that in the same way, there will be more joy in heaven over one sinner who repents than over ninety-nine righteous persons who need no repentance (Lk. 15:7).*

Perhaps the one philosophy and/or religion in the world that is the complete antithesis of true Christianity is Communism. According to fundamental Communism the individual has no intrinsic value whatsoever. The only value Communism places on the individual is in terms of whether or not they can contribute to the good of the whole. This stems from the thinking of the four men who are widely acknowledged to be the philosophical forefathers of Communism: Freud, Darwin, Huxley and Nietzsche. Each of them individually helped establish and contribute to the growing idea of their time that there was no God, and that humanity had simply evolved physically and emotionally as a result of the environment in which it found itself.

All four of them, as well as Marx and Lenin, who were shaped by their philosophies, were atheists. It was Nietzsche who stated the aphorism 'God is dead'. According to Marxism and Leninism, the individual is simply a biological by-product of a physical act between a man and woman. In fact, since Darwin's theory of 'survival of the fittest' was one of the cornerstones of Communism, the individual had only utilitarian value. That is to say, if they were weak or unproductive and could not contribute to the good of society, they were of no value. We see this reflected today in countries such as China, and in parts of India, where female babies are sometimes allowed to die soon after birth because male children are viewed as stronger and hence more able to help support the family as they get older.

The value that God places on the individual could not be more different from that of Communism. God values us for three basic but very important reasons. First, simply because we are his creation we have intrinsic value. The Genesis account of Creation says six times in the first chapter that as God looked over what he was creating he thought to himself, 'It is good.' Genesis 1:31 tells us that on the sixth day, when God saw all that he had made, 'behold, it was very good.' You and I have intrinsic value not because of our performance or our achievements, but simply because we are the craftsmanship of an incredible creator. Just as a painting by Picasso which may not be considered one of his masterpieces is still worth a great deal, even more so, a thousand times over, the least of us is of great value to God simply because we are his creation.

Secondly, we are of great value to God because each of us, as a creation of God, is a wonderful and unique reflection of God. The atheist would say you and I are only alive because of a chance occurrence of some cells joining together in the womb of a woman. To that the Bible says, 'True, but it's only part of the truth.' God created man and woman in such a way, both physically and emotionally, that they would desire each other in a sacred relationship that only two of them could share. The desire to cherish, protect and nourish that one special person in a sacred relationship of romance, commitment and friendship was intended by God to be a reflection of the love Jesus would have for his future bride, the church (Eph. 5:32).

God created marriage for two reasons. First, as a husband's or a wife's love fills a void in each of our hearts, it is to teach us of the great love Jesus has for the church and how we can respond to him. There is a void God put into the emotional and spiritual DNA of humanity that only he can fill. Secondly, it enshrines the means – love – by which God intended to continue the creation of beings made in his own image.

Although all of creation was God's handiwork, humankind has a very, very special place in his heart. And although all of God's work is good, and even very, very good, humankind is in a class of its own. That is because humankind, unlike the animal realm, is made in God's image. By that we mean that we have the capability, far beyond anything in the animal realm, to be like God, in the sense that we can reason, make choices and create. And although we could say that each and every creation in the animal realm is a special creation, it is also true that God is far more detailed in the making of each and every human being.

In his wonderful book *The Divine Romance*, Gene Edwards writes a fictionalized account of the angels watching as God created Adam. Edwards dramatically illustrates a strong curiosity on the part of the angels as to why God is putting so much care into this one particular creation. Why is God paying so much attention to this being that is so little and scrawny in comparison with the angels? Suddenly it dawns upon them that this creation, unlike all the rest, is unique in that it is made in God's image.

Psalm 139:13–15, written by David, reads:

You formed my inward parts; you wove me in my mother's womb. I will give thanks to you, for I am fearfully and wonderfully made; wonderful are your works, and my soul knows it very well. My frame was not hidden from you, when I was made in secret, and skilfully wrought in the depths of the earth.

David, the king, warrior, poet, musician and lover of God, was not giving a biology class here. Rather, he was writing out of a revelation of God's own heart and care for himself and all of humanity. In another Psalm, Asaph, who was both a seer (a prophet) and a skilled musician, wrote, 'You are gods, and all of you are sons of the Most High' (Psalm 82:6). Asaph was not saying we could become equal to God, as some have mistakenly thought. Rather, he was recognizing that as the sons and daughters of God, in the sense of being created in his image, we alone of the created realm on earth have the potential to be imitators of God: like Father, like child.

The third evidence of our unique value in God's eyes is that each human being who in faith submits his or her life to Christ and the finished work of the Cross comes into a living relationship with the Living God. As Jesus stated to Nicodemus in John chapter 3, we become 'born again'

when God's Holy Spirit comes within us. Formerly, each
of us was spiritually dead, in the sense that unless God
begins to work in our lives we are spiritually cut off from
him. But when we surrender our lives to him and trust in
Christ's payment for our sins, his Spirit begins to dwell
within our hearts and 'sonship' begins. In the premier
theological book of the New Testament, the letter to the
Romans, the Apostle Paul wrote:

> *For you have not received a spirit of slavery leading to fear again,*
> *but you have received a spirit of adoption as sons by which we cry*
> *out, 'Abba! Father!' (Rom. 8:15).*

When the Holy Spirit comes into our hearts, he brings
us into a father/child relationship with God. And this
'sonship' is not only for men, but for both men and women.
When we come to Christ Jesus as our Lord and Saviour,
each of us, whether man or woman, becomes in effect the
oldest son who has the full inheritance. In fact, Paul went
on to say that we are 'co-heirs' with Christ (Rom. 8:17,
NIV).

Paul's statement that we have not received a spirit of
slavery leading us into a relationship of fear, but rather a
spirit of adoption, is at the very heart of the Gospel. God
does not value us on the basis of our successes in life or our
contributions to the work of the Kingdom. God values each
one of us who comes to Christ simply because we are now
his son or his daughter. His love for us is an unconditional
love; our relationship is not performance-oriented. We are
of immense value simply because of who we are to him.
This understanding might prompt us to ask, 'Why then
should a Christian live sacrificially, if there's nothing to
earn or prove?' The answer is simple. If we have truly
given our lives to God, and his own Spirit is now in our
hearts, his nature will begin to emerge, as opposed to the

nature of carnality. We begin to learn to love and serve sacrificially because that is the very nature of God. As Acts 20:35 says, in words attributed to Jesus, 'It is more blessed to give than to receive.'

It is only in our fallen state of grace that we rate one another and ourselves according to our performance, success and outward appearance. It is not so in heaven, neither was it that way in the Garden before sin entered the picture. In Adam's very first words to God after his and Eve's disobedience, he casts blame on the woman. The devastating effect of sin is twofold: separ-ation from God, and division between humans. The syndrome of rating, blaming and scapegoating affects almost every area of our lives. Only the Cross and the love of God have the potential to set us free by restoring us to a relationship of significance and security with our Maker.

As the saying goes, God hates sin but loves sinners. He hates sin because it is rebellion and it breeds destruction. He loves sinners, however, because we are his creation and we are made in his image, with the potential of being like him. For those two reasons alone God is committed to healing broken lives. God loves to heal his sons and daughters, as a good father would. And nowhere is there more anointing for physical healing than in the context of expressing and extending the Kingdom of God. As we saw in the first chapter, Jesus instructed the disciples (the church) to preach the Gospel of the Kingdom, cast out demons and heal the sick. When God's healing power goes forth, it is both the evidence of his love for hurting people and the destruction of the work of the devil, who came to rob kill and destroy. The first letter of John says:

The Son of God appeared for this purpose, to destroy the works of the devil (1 Jn. 3:8).

God is in the healing business, to restore all the wonderful works of art that the great vandal and thief, the devil, has tried to mar and steal.

Seeing beyond the outward appearance

'Man looks at the outward appearance, but the LORD looks at the heart,' God said to Samuel the prophet (1 Sam. 16:7). We are so entrenched in the ratings game that it is difficult for us, apart from the love of God, to value one another simply for who we are. In the workplace in particular we can't help but value one another for our performance. And while it is true that an employee who can achieve more is usually of more value to his or her employer, we tend to use that same measuring stick for almost all of life. Our culture teaches young girls that they must be pretty to be valued. We teach boys that if they are better at sports they are more valued. The whole grading system of most schools reinforces the idea that the high achievers are 'better' than the average or low achievers.

My ministry uses a charge card to pay our extensive airline bills, so we receive a free monthly magazine which typically focuses on very expensive hotels, clothes and other items. Glancing through it recently, I noticed an advertisement for a men's blazer that cost $3,600. I couldn't help laughing to myself. Not that there was anything wrong with someone who could afford such an expensive casual jacket purchasing it. It just struck me that 99 per cent of the world's population would never even dream of spending that much on a mere garment. The message that all the articles, pictures and advertisements in that magazine give is that there is a certain class of people who have 'arrived' in life, by virtue of their affluent lifestyle. All the models and people shown in its pictures personify the rich and the beautiful. The average person will never be featured in an advertisement or article in that magazine. Does that mean that he or she is of no value, or has no beauty? Absolutely not.

God looks at the unsuccessful in the game of life. He looks at the not so beautiful and the poor. He looks at the lame, the diseased and the scarred and says, 'You have worth to me.' In his great love he says, 'The Lord takes pleasure in his people; he will beautify the afflicted ones with salvation' (Ps. 149:4). The singer / songwriter Nichole Nordeman powerfully illustrates the great contrast between God's value system and the world's in her song 'Anyway'. She sings of God calling her beautiful even though her shame was so evident. She continues with being placed on the wall of God's great gallery of fine art anyway! Or, as Isaiah the prophet put it, God longs to give us 'beauty for ashes' (Is. 61:3 KJV).

The movie *Seabiscuit* features a recurring line, first used in relation to a horse that is prized by an old cowboy. The cowboy, played by Chris Cooper, has turned to training racehorses because the open ranges he used to ride have been fenced in with barbed wire. Others at the horse track refer to him as an 'old crackpot'. A rich potential customer asks why he cares so much for a particular horse that's been physically damaged and can no longer race. He responds, 'You don't throw a whole life away just because he's banged up a little.' The movie is a powerful demonstration of value in the life of the cowboy, the wealthy businessman, a young jockey and the future champion racehorse called Seabiscuit. All are at a stage in their lives where in their own eyes or the eyes of others they are broken failures. The message of the movie is not just about moving from failure to success; it is about truly valuing ourselves and others.

In the cultures of the world too many people are seen as having little worth. Even worse, many are seen as dispensable because they have nothing to offer that's considered valuable. In the eyes of God, however, each and every human being is not only of great value but also of potential beauty and purpose. Isaiah said that God wants to give us 'beauty instead of ashes' (Is. 61:3, NIV). God wants to restore us to the potential and splendour of simply being his creation. Much as a master violin-maker might look at a damaged Stradivarius violin and view it as precious despite the damage, so God the Father looks at hurting and broken people and sees them as being of priceless value.

Our God-given personalities, our physical attributes and our intellectual abilities are all gifts from God. And no matter how different we are one from another, God sees each of us as the apple of his eye. When he sees our flaws, hurts and failures, rather than viewing us as rubbish to discard, he reaches out to us with an unquenchable love.

To the evolutionist we are simply a chance being in a chance world. The wonder of our make-up, however, denies that. As some have said before, the mathematical probability of a human evolving from a slug over millions of years is less than that of an ape manufacturing a perfectly built jumbo jet out of scrapyard parts. The mind and body of a human, with all their complexity and potential, are too wonderful simply to have evolved. The human adult body has some 206 bones, which work so amazingly well together. The human hand itself has 26 bones, which allow humans to design, create and build in a way no animal could, even if their brains were capable of it.

The human mind is an absolutely amazing thing. It contains some 100 billion neurons, or nerve cells, that travel at speeds of up to 200 miles per hour. Of course, most animals that live in the wild respond and react much more quickly and with more agility than a human can. But only the human mind, which was created in God's image, can process abstract thoughts and do complex problem-solving. When it comes to creativity, birds, for example, are wonderfully adept at building nests which can enable their family to survive a winter. Only the human mind, however, could envision and produce the plans and technology for something as simple as a wheel, let alone a car, motorcycle, ship or space rocket. Moreover, even though many animals have a sense of self-awareness, only the human mind has the capacity for reflective thinking over both the past and the future. As wonderful a tool as computers can be, with their ability to store facts and knowledge, they fall far short of the wonder of the human mind. And of course, let us not forget that as wonderful as computers are, they were created by humans.

The human mind, body and soul are precious to God. First, simply because we are his creation and therefore have great intrinsic value. God put far more care into our creation than into all the rest of the earth's inhabitants. The care with which we are made and the Godlike potential within each of us sets us apart from the animal realm. Secondly, God has made each of us to be a unique reflection of himself. Each human is a work of art. The tragedy of our fallen state is that we so easily defile ourselves and others. And last but not least, when we receive Christ as our Lord and Saviour, we become adopted as a prize son or daughter by God the Father. God is into the healing business because he loves us, but also because each of us is a wonderful and unique creation highly valued by the Creator himself.

Therefore the LORD longs to be gracious to you, and therefore he waits on high to have compassion on you. For the LORD is a God of justice; how blessed are all those who long for him (Is. 30:18).

Chapter 4

Models of Healing Prayer

MARK STIBBE

Given that God longs to heal the sick, what kind of models of divine healing are best suited to the task of bringing his compassion to hurting people?

The church I lead, St Andrew's Chorleywood, built and consecrated in 1966, has had a rich history as regards divine healing. The first vicar, Revd John Perry, heard about the move of God's Holy Spirit in the Episcopalian Church in the USA and started weekly prayer meetings seeking more of God's Holy Spirit. Both he and many of the people of St Andrew's were subsequently filled with the Holy Spirit and the church began to grow significantly. One of the major areas of growth was in the healing ministry. John encouraged a sacramental method of healing prayer, with prayer taking place at the altar rails during Holy Communion. The leaders of the church, including non-ordained people, prayed for the sick with the laying-on of hands. Many people were healed through this kind of prayer during the 1970s.

In the late 1970s, a new vicar arrived to take John's place: Bishop David Pytches. He heard from David Watson about a church leader in the USA who had seen phenomenal church growth through evangelism with signs and wonders. The man's name was John Wimber. David dared to invite John to St Andrew's for the Pentecost weekend of 1981. John brought a large team of young people at his own expense and, during that weekend, he and the team ministered to the church. That visit changed St Andrew's profoundly. There was a powerful outpouring of the Holy Spirit (the second in its short history) and the church went into another phase of renewal and growth.

Once again the ministry of divine healing was a prominent feature. In this new phase of the church's history, the method employed owed everything to John Wimber's teaching. It involved a simple five-step procedure that anyone was able to use, not just the officers of the church. The emphasis was on inviting the Holy Spirit to come and then following his lead. During David Pytches' ministry (which ended when I was appointed vicar in 1996), it would be no exaggeration to say that hundreds experienced healing at St Andrew's, maybe even thousands. We still use the method John Wimber introduced at St Andrew's today.

Models of divine healing

A question frequently asked by those wanting to learn about healing concerns method. What is the right way to pray for the sick? There are so many different types of healing ministry in the church. Which one is best suited for continued use, year in and year out, in the local church?

Perhaps the best thing to do before answering this question is to remind ourselves of the various models of healing prayer that have been evident in the church over the last two thousand years.

Ronald Kydd has provided an overview of these in his book *Healing Through the Centuries*. Kydd points out that Jesus himself did not operate with just one model of healing prayer but used a variety of methods. Indeed, Jesus' ministry generally did not involve patterns or formulas. So Kydd urges us to be cautious about trying to tie healing down to just one method. For him, healing is a mystery and 'the claim to have understood healing is evidence that one has not'.

Having said that, Kydd does believe it is possible to identify a number of different models of healing prayer used throughout the centuries. He makes the very telling point that the effective use of these models by various Christians cannot be used as proof of their theological 'soundness' or orthodoxy. Augustine realized this many centuries ago when he said, 'Not only do the good and bad perform miracles but sometimes the good perform them not.'

Kydd identifies six major models of healing prayer in church history. The first is 'the **confrontational** model'. Here the central theme is the Kingdom of God and the main idea is one of 'confrontation' between God's rule and the kingdom of darkness. In this model, healing prayer is seen as a manifestation of God's reign on earth. When healing occurs, it is an example of a victorious power encounter with the devil's works. Kydd points to early church fathers such as Irenaeus, Tertullian, Cyprian and Origen as proponents of this model. More recently he points to J. C. Blumhardt and John Wimber.

The second model Kydd identifies is what he calls 'the **intercessory** model'. This model is characterized by praying to various 'saints', and is common in Orthodox and Roman Catholic circles. It is in fact closely linked with the wider practice of the veneration of 'saints'. The idea behind this model is that the ministry of certain 'super-Christians' continues after their death. Ambrose, Bishop of Milan, was the first to propose such an idea but it was not until four hundred years later, with the teaching of John of Damascus, that the idea became popular. He used the metaphor of the 'patron' to justify this idea. Just as a patron can introduce you to a king and speak on your behalf, so the saints function as mediators and intercessors before the King of Kings. Kydd looks at Brother André as a more contemporary example of the intercessory model, and Mary of Medjugorje (in which the dominant idea revolves around Mary as intercessor).

In the third part of Kydd's study he introduces us to what he calls 'the **reliquarial** model'. Those who employ this particular model of healing believe that miracles come through the use of the 'relics' or remains of especially revered Christians of the past. These relics can be bodily (bones), instrumental (the things used by various saints) or representative (such as tombs). Kydd shows that this particular model is foreign to most Protestants and is more common in the Orthodox and Roman Catholic traditions. Regard for the physical remains of early Christian martyrs goes back to the time of Irenaeus, who died in Rome in or around the year AD 117. However, it is not until the fourth and fifth centuries that relics start to feature in acts of worship. Even Augustine admitted this practice. He wrote, 'The truth is that even today miracles are being wrought in the name of Christ, sometimes through his sacraments and sometimes through the intercession of the relics of the saints' (*City of God*, chapter 8, book 22). By the Middle Ages, the importance of relics was well established. Shrines were set up where direct contact with relics was thought to bring about miraculous healing. Kydd points to the miracles reported at St Médard in Paris (eighteenth century) as a more contemporary example.

The fourth approach Kydd calls 'the **incubational** model'. Here the image of the incubator suggests a nurturing and hospitable environment where healing occurs over time. With the incubational model we come to the idea of divine healing as something that happens in certain centres and gradually rather than suddenly. The incubational model stresses improvement over the course of time. Usually the context is a residential home or retreat centre for the sick. Marguerite Chapuis said, 'Healing ... is rarely instantaneous. It is the fruit of persevering prayer.' While Kydd cannot point to this practice in the early church, he draws attention to contemporary examples in Mannedorf, south of Zurich, and Yverdon-les-Bains, near Lausanne.

The fifth approach Kydd calls 'the **revelational** model'. Here the dominant idea concerns the importance of utter dependence upon God in the healing ministry. If healing is to happen, God must lead those who are praying for the sick by giving them prophetic revelation concerning who to pray for and how to pray for them. In this model, healing is not so much a process (as in the incubational model) as a crisis. It happens suddenly, when God imparts special knowledge to those doing the praying. Kydd again does not provide examples from church history prior to the twentieth century. He focuses on the healing ministries of William Branham and Kathryn Kuhlman to illustrate the model.

The final approach Kydd describes is what he calls 'the **soteriological** model'. Soteriology literally means 'the study or doctrine of salvation'. Salvation of course comes to us through the finished work of Christ on the Cross. This work is called the 'atonement', the means by which God in Christ enabled estranged human beings to be 'at one' with him. In the soteriological model, the Cross is absolutely central. Here the slogan is 'healing is in the atonement'. In other words, the Cross not only provides us with the forgiveness of our sins; it also provides us with the healing of our bodies. Kydd rightly points to Pentecostalism as the place where this model has been emphasized most strongly and focuses on Oral Roberts as his primary example.

Assessing the models

Looking at these models from a Pentecostal or a Charismatic perspective, one is likely to find some more appealing than others. The idea of using relics as a means of acquiring divine healing is not one that is encouraged in the ministry of Jesus or the New Testament as a whole, and is therefore not particularly congenial to someone wanting a Bible-based approach. Praying to the saints or to Mary rather than to the Father will also strike many of us as something strange and lacking in biblical foundation. Similarly, while healing can often be a process (the incubational model), Pentecostals and Charismatics are more likely to press in for healing that is immediate, as it was for the most part in the ministry of Jesus and the first Christians.

At the same time, to adapt a quotation from Shakespeare's *Hamlet*, there are more things in heaven and earth than are dreamt of in our Pentecostal and Charismatic theologies. God is in the business of doing unexpected things. He is also the God of 'incarnation', the God who accommodates himself to us and communicates in an idiom we can understand. Sometimes divine healing takes place in ways and environments that are not what some of us would regard as natural to our particular beliefs.

To take one example from my own life, two years ago I found myself teaching in a vibrant Charismatic church in Perth, Western Australia. The church has grown to about three thousand and is a dramatic example of the power of

God. Yet the thing I remember most about that visit was not the meetings in church but being taken by the senior pastor to a small house on an estate outside the city. There the mother of one of the church leaders had a statue of Mary that was weeping oil. With my own eyes I saw this and indeed videoed it. The University of Perth had asked if they could examine the statue and had inspected it for a week. When they had finished, they could not arrive at an explanation as to why this statue was weeping fragrant oil. That was their way of saying that science could not explain this phenomenon.

What was interesting here was that the statue clearly had some association with divine healing. The mother in question had set up an altar in her front room with a Cross at the centre and the statue of Mary to one side (so as not to obscure the central importance of Jesus). By the time I visited, thousands of Roman Catholics had made pilgrimage to this room and hundreds had been challenged to get right with God and return to him. Others had received significant healing. One six-year-old girl, who had never spoken in her life, on visiting this makeshift shrine had her tongue released to speak for the first time in her life. That occurred the week before I visited.

Now, I am not in a position to say categorically that this is genuine or false. I am frankly undecided. However, if it is genuine, this is a warning to us that some of the models Kydd identifies, though they may feel strange to some of us, may nevertheless be used to secure divine healing for those who can only find God in such a spirituality or environment. While this is not an endorsement of heresy, generosity as well as discernment is required when examining models of healing with which we are personally unfamiliar.

Kydd's summary is therefore quite helpful for assessing which models of divine healing may be viable in a local church setting. Anyone wanting to establish a ministry of healing in the local church can look at Kydd's overview and assess which of these is most user-friendly and sustainable. From a Pentecostal and Charismatic perspective, the models that are most likely to appeal are the confrontational, revelational and soteriological models. The idea of using relics in the local church is not practical and would certainly be regarded as unbiblical by some. The practice of asking various saints to function as mediators and intercessors would also certainly flounder for theological reasons. The incubational model has a lot to commend it because it encourages us to see the local church as a community of healing. At the same time, it militates against the idea that divine healing often happens suddenly, not just gradually.

In what follows I want to change Kydd's categories and talk about two models, 'the Kingdom model' and 'the faith model'. These two roughly correspond to what Kydd calls the 'confrontational' and the 'soteriological' models respectively. I have chosen to highlight these two models because they are the ones with which most Pentecostals and Charismatics are currently grappling. This is not to imply that there aren't other models worthy of attention. But these two are the dominant paradigms in contemporary Pentecostal and Charismatic circles. In the 'Kingdom model' we will be concentrating on John Wimber. In the 'faith model' we will be concentrating on Roger Sapp. In both we will evaluate the strengths and weaknesses for prayer ministry in the local church.

The Kingdom model

I remember well my first introduction to John Wimber. It was 1985 and I had heard about his ministry from many quarters. At the time I was reading theology and training for the ordained ministry in Nottingham. Everything I was reading about the healing ministry of Jesus seemed to be endorsing the sceptical, liberal view that the miracles of Jesus did not really happen but are symbolic stories. At the time I had no personal experience of divine healing, so I was somewhat infected by this dismissive perspective. However, I was about to learn how wrong this was.

In 1985 John Wimber came to the city of Sheffield, about an hour's drive north of Nottingham. He brought a team with him to teach on signs and wonders and the Kingdom of God. At the time I was in a small prayer group with three other men training for ordained ministry. These three were more experienced than I in the whole area of divine healing. They signed up for the conference in Sheffield and signed me up too, reasoning that I needed to be exposed to the miraculous. When I found out, I was somewhat ambivalent. I was angry that they felt I so desperately needed such input and at the same time pleased that they wanted to include me!

A few months later, the four of us duly travelled an hour up the motorway to the city hall in Sheffield for a four-day conference. After registering, we sat with three thousand other delegates in the huge auditorium, waiting for John Wimber to appear. The music group led us in the most intimate and beautiful worship I had ever experienced in nearly ten years as a Christian. Then, after forty-five minutes, John Wimber came on stage – a large, white-haired, bearded, grandfatherly figure. He preached for nearly an hour on the Kingdom of God in the teaching and ministry of Jesus, stressing what I had already been taught in my theological studies, that the Kingdom is absolutely central to the message of Jesus.

John Wimber taught then, and over the subsequent sessions, that Jesus had come to usher in the dynamic reign of almighty God in human history. What the Jewish people of Jesus' day had thought would come at the end of history had now arrived in the here and now. To be sure, the Kingdom of God will only be fully established on the earth in the Second Coming of Jesus, when all things will be in subjection to Jesus Christ in the new heaven and the new earth. In the meantime, we live in the tension between the 'already' and the 'not yet' – between Jesus' first coming and the inauguration of God's Kingdom, and Jesus' second coming, and the consummation of God's Kingdom. This interim period is characterized by intense spiritual warfare between God's increasing, growing and expanding Kingdom, and the retreating kingdom of darkness.

In this time-frame between the first and second comings of Jesus, the church's responsibility is to continue the ministry of Jesus. The church is the body of Christ on the earth. Through the power of the Holy Spirit, churches everywhere can continue to do what Jesus did. In practice this means extending the Kingdom of God. Jesus did this in his earthly life through preaching the message of the Kingdom and through performing miracles that demonstrated the Kingdom. It is this combination of message and miracles, proclamation and demonstration, that the church is called to make a priority today. Every believer is called to this task.

The Kingdom of God is therefore the key to divine healing. Healing is a manifestation of the reign of God. It involves a power encounter between God's rule and Satan's works, specifically his works of sin, sickness, suffering and death. At the same time, the Kingdom is not yet fully established on the earth. This means that there are times when we do not see God's rule expressed in the complete way we would like. As John himself put it:

The fact that we are living between the first and second comings of Christ, what George Ladd calls living between the 'already and the not yet', provides the interpretative key for understanding why the physical healing that Christ secured for us in or through the atonement is not always experienced today (*Power Evangelism*, p. 169).

The Kingdom model and divine healing

At the conference in Sheffield, John Wimber introduced a simple model of divine healing prayer. He not only taught it, he also demonstrated it.

In *Power Healing*, his follow-up book to *Power Evangelism*, John Wimber wrote two chapters on what he called the 'healing procedure'. This involved five steps that John saw in the ministry of Jesus, though he admitted that the steps are not presented in a systematic or chronological way in Scripture. He wrote:

> The five-step procedure may be used at any time and in any place: in hotels, at neighbours' homes, on aeroplanes, at the office and, of course, in church gatherings. I have been in casual conversations with people, even complete strangers, who mention some physical condition, and I ask, 'May I pray for you?' Rarely do they decline healing prayer, even if they are not Christians. I then confidently pray for them by following the five-step method.

The five steps consist of the following:

Step One: the interview. This simply involves asking the person, 'What do you want me to pray for?' As the person replies, the ones ministering are encouraged to listen not only to what the person is saying but also to what the Father is saying. This double listening is a key characteristic of the five-step model.

Step Two: the diagnosis. In this part of the procedure those ministering are asking the question, 'Why does this person have this condition?' There is a lot of overlap with the first step here. The insight one has been asking for in the interview stage here forms part of the diagnostic decision. This insight comes through words of knowledge, words of wisdom and the discernment of spirits. In other words, the revelatory gifts of the Spirit often provide the right diagnosis. This does not have to be the case, however. John himself said that he always found it easier to ask questions than think he had to receive words of knowledge. But he found that sometimes God revealed the real need that the person had (and this could contradict the person's stated need).

Step Three: prayer selection. This step involves answering the question, 'What kind of prayer is needed to help this person?' John believed, like Francis MacNutt, that there are essentially four kinds of healing. These were first introduced in MacNutt's classic book *Healing* (Hodder & Stoughton), a copy of which was given by John Wimber to every one of the three thousand delegates at the Sheffield conference in 1985. MacNutt describes them on page 163 of his book:

1. Prayer for repentance (for personal sin)
2. Prayer for inner healing (for emotional hurts)
3. Prayer for physical healing
4. Prayer for deliverance

These correspond to the three different kinds of sickness: spiritual, emotional and physical. Prayer selection involves asking God, 'Do you want me to pray for healing right now?' If the answer is 'Yes', the next question is 'How?' 'In which of the four ways above?'

Step Four: prayer engagement. This consists of praying with the laying-on of hands for the person in need. The way one prays is determined by the diagnosis and the prayer selection (steps two and three). Crucial to this step is inviting the Holy Spirit to come and release his healing power. As the prayer continues, there are sometimes manifestations of the Holy Spirit. These may include crying, laughing, fluttering eyelids, shaking, drunkenness, falling over and so on. Such manifestations do not always happen, and John was at pains to stress that they are not a *necessary* accompaniment of the Holy Spirit's action. What John found most common was the need for confession of sin. He discovered in his wide experience that breakthroughs in healing often came when sin was acknowledged in a sick person's life. Prayer engagement therefore nearly always involved leading a person in confessing their sin before God and receiving his forgiveness, so that further healing work could take place. Repentance, in short, is critical.

Step Five: post-prayer direction. Here the important question is, 'What must the person do if they are to keep their healing?' Another important question might be, 'What should this person do if they are not healed here and now?' Those who are healed are told to sin no more in order to keep their healing. Those who are not healed are reminded of the Father's love for them and encouraged to go on seeking more prayer.

Evaluating the Kingdom model

The central theme of John Wimber's teaching was accordingly the central theme of Jesus' teaching, namely, the Kingdom of God. Everything John taught about divine healing arose out of his understanding of the Kingdom.

This meant that God was and is always sovereign in the matter of healing. As John wrote in *Power Healing*:

> God's sovereignty, lordship and kingdom are what bring healing. Our part is to pray, 'Thy kingdom come' – and trust him for whatever healing comes from his gracious hand (p. 169).

What are we to make of this Kingdom model?

I would like to begin by making five positive comments about John's model of healing prayer.

First, John's teaching was totally grounded in the Bible. Everything he taught had a sound biblical basis. In his book *Power Healing* he states, 'Scripture must always be the primary source and basis for our practice' (p. 11). I have never been able to find a major fault scripturally with John's teaching. None of it involved fanciful exegesis. All of it revolved around the plain meaning of Scripture and particularly the Gospels.

Secondly, John's teaching was thoroughly Christ-centred. Everything he taught had its roots in the ministry and message of Jesus Christ. In many ways, John's teaching was more scriptural and Christ-centred than anything else I had heard in evangelical circles up to that point. Instead of ignoring the more 'supernatural parts of the Bible', John treated those parts as authoritative and relevant for us today.

Thirdly, John's teaching was motivated by a desire to help the church evangelize a lost world more effectively. John's main book was called *Power Evangelism*. His whole emphasis was on getting back to the New Testament model of witnessing, which involved the power of the Holy Spirit as well as proclaiming the Gospel. His heart beat with incredible fervency for mission. He had seen thousands come to Christ in his own ministry through power evangelism. He desperately wanted churches everywhere to be equipped to do what Jesus did – to combine proclamation and demonstration in evangelizing unbelievers.

Fourthly, John's teaching was transferable to the local church. John taught and modelled a way of praying for the sick that could be reproduced in any local church situation over any length of time. John's great vision was to empower ordinary Christians to believe they have the authority to minister healing. In my own church the model introduced by John Wimber is still proving extremely effective after nearly twenty years in operation. In a recent feedback meeting with our healing prayer ministry team the following were reported:

- A lady healed of migraines
- A lady healed of a thyroid condition
- A person healed of phobias of snakes and heights
- A man who was schizophrenic and had to be in a padded cell most of the time was brought by his mother to St Andrew's twenty years ago. He was prayed for and the Lord miraculously healed him. This healing has only just been reported. He is now living in his own home in the community. The miracle is acknowledged by friends and specialists.
- Cancer patients freed of pain
- A girl from a mental hospital experienced healing
- A person with perforated eardrum healed
- A chipped knee healed
- A number of knees healed
- A leg lengthened and hip realigned
- A back healed during worship
- A person received deliverance

- Someone whose husband died six weeks ago was given a word ('Jesus is your bridegroom') by the ministry team member. She was greatly encouraged.

Finally, John's teaching was pastoral. John never taught that everyone is healed as we pray for the sick. His theology of the Kingdom allowed for the possibility that some prayers would be answered with a 'not yet' rather than a 'now'. Speaking frankly, having been a pastor in four churches now, I am so glad that I adopted this view rather than the 'always now' approach. We have to respect the mystery as well as the majesty of the Kingdom of God. In this respect, John would have agreed wholeheartedly with Derek Morphew's words (which I have already cited) in his book *Breakthrough: Discovering the Kingdom*:

> We can say categorically that healing occurs because the kingdom of God breaks through. We can say equally categorically that healing does not always occur because the kingdom of God has not broken through finally. No one can say what determines how frequently and on what basis this intervention of the powers of the age to come takes place. This is the mystery of the kingdom.

At the same time, criticisms have been levelled against John's Kingdom model. Some of these have been unfair and often expressed by people who neither knew John nor attended his meetings. Nevertheless, one fair criticism concerns the diagnostic stage of the five-step model. Recent advocates of what has been called 'the person-centred model of healing' have criticized John for making the sick person too passive. They argue that the use of the word 'diagnosis' makes the one ministering a doctor figure and the sick person a patient. The person-centred model is an attempt to remedy this shortcoming insofar as it encourages a far greater level of involvement from the sick person. They are not simply passive, but rather they are urged to lead the process by answering the question, 'How would you like God to come to you right now?' Further questions are asked that invite the person to actually picture God in relation to them.

Speaking personally, I do not believe that the person-centred model is an adequate or necessary replacement for the Kingdom model. I also believe that the case made against the five-step procedure, especially the diagnostic step, is overstated, though it is not without grounds. John's description of the procedure does in fact involve asking questions of the sick person, as my summary above clearly shows. The sick person is by no means as passive as John's critics make out. Having said that, I do agree that more emphasis should be placed on the sick person's participation. I also agree that 'words of knowledge' are not a *sine qua non* for the procedure to work. I have in any case questioned John's definition of the 'word of knowledge' in my book *Prophetic Evangelism*, arguing that what John called 'the word of knowledge' is really 'personal prophecy'.

So the Kingdom model is not flawless, as John himself had the humility to admit. He believed that a Reformed church is always reforming. Therefore he expected there to be growth in this model. However, I would submit that John's model is still one of the most astute and practical.

The faith model of healing prayer

If the Kingdom model of healing prayer is more common in Charismatic churches, the 'faith model' has historically been more visible in Pentecostal circles. The faith model starts with the example of Jesus. It stresses that Jesus healed every single sick person that came to him asking to be made well. If Jesus Christ is the Son who truly reveals the Father, this tells us something about God. It tells us that God's will is always to heal every sick person. Put in the form of a syllogism, the reasoning goes thus:

> Jesus Christ reveals what God the Father is like.
>
> Jesus Christ healed every sick person who asked.
>
> Therefore God wants every sick person to be well.

Another key foundation stone in the faith model concerns the Cross. Those who endorse the faith model argue that Jesus died not just to forgive us our sins but also to heal our bodies. Jesus died for the whole person.

Vital to this argument are three scriptures that have often been quoted in this regard. First of all, Isaiah 53:4–5, where the prophet says:

> *Yet it was our weaknesses he carried; it was our sorrows that weighed him down. And we thought his troubles were a punishment from God for his own sins! But he was wounded and crushed for our sins. He was beaten that we might have peace. He was whipped, and we were healed!*

Here Isaiah, prophesying the events of Calvary six hundred years before they occurred, states that Jesus died not only as a substitute for our sins but also for our 'healing'. This theme is further taken up by Matthew in chapter 8 of his Gospel, when he says:

> *That evening many demon-possessed people were brought to Jesus. All the spirits fled when he commanded them to leave; and he healed all the sick. This fulfilled the word of the Lord through Isaiah, who said, 'He took our sicknesses and removed our diseases'* (Mt. 8:16–17).

The same idea relationship between the Cross and healing seems to be suggested by the Apostle Peter in chapter 2 of his first letter:

> *He personally carried away our sins in his own body on the cross so we can be dead to sin and live for what is right. You have been healed by his wounds! (1 Pet. 2:24).*

All this is central to the proponents of the faith model. They argue that we have to embrace the truth that healing is the atoning work of the Cross and that if we do it will produce consistent results in healing ministry. They contend that the Bible passages above are quite sufficient to argue that healing is in the atonement to the same degree that forgiveness of sins is. The clear implication of this formula is that healing is in the Cross and all we have to do is confess it to possess it.

All this serves to highlight the critical role of faith in the process. The idea is that we only have to believe and we will receive our healing. Just as we believed God for our salvation, so we can believe God for healing. People become Christians when *they* decide to believe. *They* choose to come to faith. They take the initiative, not God. Similarly, with healing, people are healed when they choose to believe that healing belongs to them because of the Cross. They choose, not God. They take the initiative, not God. Therefore divine healing is not the result of God deciding out of his own free will to bless someone. It is the result of a sick person (and those praying for him or her) believing for what is already guaranteed at the Cross.

For the faith preachers divine healing should therefore be automatic and immediate. Just as we automatically received forgiveness when we believed in what Jesus had done at Calvary, so we should automatically receive healing when we believe in the finished work of the Cross.

The main reason why people do not receive immediately is lack of faith. In such situations we need to persist in prayer until they get the breakthrough.

Evaluating the faith model

There are positive things to learn from this 'faith model' of healing prayer. First of all, those who hold it are right to begin with Jesus. Jesus healed all those who came to him asking to be made well. It is also vital to remember that this in itself reveals that God is a good Father who wants us to be well. As Ken Blue has powerfully argued, in one of the best written yet least read books on healing (*Authority to Heal*), 'Erroneous views of healing arise out of erroneous views of God.' The idea that God desires us to be ill, so that we can somehow be sanctified through sickness, is not taught by Jesus. Jesus never treated people's sicknesses as something good, God-sent or redemptive. He saw them as evil. This tells us something about God. As Ken Blue reminds us, 'Openly receiving healing for ourselves and confidently praying for others rests ultimately on our understanding of who God is' (p. 70).

Secondly, faith preachers are right to remind us of the centrality of the Cross in the healing ministry. John Wimber believed that healing was one of the benefits of the Cross but he would not preach that healing was 'in' the atonement. Faith preachers believe that healing is in the atonement and accordingly give centre stage to the Calvary event. The positive effect of this Cross-centred theology is that it reminds us of the importance of sharing the message of the Cross whenever we minister divine healing. We are called to preach the Gospel. If we disconnect the healing ministry from the Gospel, we deny people the whole Gospel and minister only in part.

Thirdly, there is no doubt we all need challenging when it comes to faith. Speaking for myself, I know I could do with believing for far more when it comes to divine healing. Faith preachers can spur us on to believe that God can do far more than we have seen so far. Those who emphasize faith have much to teach us. They are certainly closer to the truth than those who believe and preach that healing is not available to people at all. As Ken Blue says:

> Evangelical Christians claim to believe the Bible, and we do regarding the historical events it records. We have faith in what Jesus did two thousand years ago, but we are often crippled with doubt when asked to believe what he might do today (p. 99).

At the same time, there are weaknesses in the faith model of divine healing. Yes, Jesus Christ reveals the Father, and his healing ministry must show us that God wants us well, not sick. But Ken Blue puts it in a far more judicious way when he writes, 'God wills the ultimate healing of all spiritual, psychological and physical sickness' (p. 69). The key word to underline is the word 'ultimate'. Yes, God's general and ultimate will is for all sicknesses to be eradicated. Jesus Christ clearly reveals this. But does this means that it is always his specific and immediate will to eradicate all sickness in every individual situation that we meet today? That is a big leap theologically. While it seems to be relentlessly logical, in actual experience no one finds this to be the case.

Secondly, I am completely convinced that divine healing is one of the blessings of the atonement. But does this mean that healing is as available as justification? I don't think so. The best interpreter of Scripture is Scripture. While the passages in Isaiah 53, Matthew 8 and 1 Peter 2 may appear to say that Christ died for our sicknesses as well as our sins (and there is still a good deal of debate about whether they do), the New Testament as a whole does not give any indication that healing is as available to us as pardon for sin. If you take the letters of Paul, you can find no teaching on this at all. Paul's emphasis all the time is on the Cross as the place where the guilty are made righteous. There is no hint in his writings that he believed that healing was in the atonement to the same degree that forgiveness of sins is. This leads me to the inevitable conclusion that healing is indeed one of the many benefits of the finished work of the Cross. However, it is a secondary, not a primary, benefit. That is not in any way to minimize its importance. It is simply to say that divine healing takes second place to the forgiveness of sins.

Thirdly, the emphasis on faith has a downside to it. The idea that believing is the key to receiving means that there is no really pastoral way of explaining why people do not get healed. The only possible conclusion is that someone somewhere did not have sufficient faith. Almost inevitably this means blaming the person who needs prayer, and this results in them feeling worse than they did before they were prayed for. The pastoral consequences of the faith model are therefore potentially disastrous in a local church. We have operated an effective ministry of divine healing for the ten years that I have been vicar of St Andrew's Chorleywood. But during that time we have seen some people die of their sicknesses. Why is that? Here we have to fall back on what Derek Morphew calls the 'mystery of the Kingdom'. As Kathryn Kuhlman, one of the most effective proponents of the faith model, once said:

Twenty years ago I believed that absolutely, come hell or high water, it was God's will for everybody, without exception, to be healed. But I've watched this thing very carefully. Now I see that we can't demand or command that God do anything. In general, I definitely believe that it is God's will to heal. But I can't say absolutely what is or is not his will in a particular case. There are some things I've learned just not to touch.

The faith model therefore has some merits, but it is not a model that is sustainable in the local church. Sooner or later pastors and people are going to run into the mystery of why some are not healed, even after persistent and faithful prayer. The Pentecostal faith paradigm is therefore of limited value. In fact, it is even rejected today by most Pentecostals. A recent questionnaire of British Pentecostal ministers revealed the following:

Distribution of non-faith-teaching and faith-teaching ministries by age		
Age	'No' to faith model	'Yes' to faith model
Under 34	82.2%	17.8%
35–49	81.2%	18.8%
50–64	68.6%	31.4%
Over 65	61.5%	38.5%

The findings suggest that some of the older generation of British Pentecostal ministers still hold on to the 'faith model' of healing, while the majority of younger and middle-aged ministers have now rejected it.

Contrasting the two models

In conclusion, it is important to note the differences between the two models of healing prayer. A key here lies in understanding the two ideas of God's freedom and God's faithfulness. An extreme view of God's faithfulness would argue that his promise in Scripture is to heal everyone and he is faithful in that. An extreme view of God's freedom would state that God is free to choose how and when to act and this is totally mysterious. The healing theology of John Wimber leans more towards a theology of God's freedom. In John's understanding, God is sovereign and his purposes are sometimes mysterious.

God has nowhere in the Bible committed himself to promising healing every time a sick person requests prayer. Therefore he is not bound by necessity to answer every request for a healing with a YES, NOW. He may answer YES and give the healing NOW. But he is also free in his sovereignty to say NOT YET, and wait until the new heaven and the new earth, when all sickness will disappear and God will wipe away every tear from our eyes. On that day, all believers will experience the ultimate and most wonderful healing.

The healing theology of the faith preachers is quite different from this. They lean far more towards a theology of God's faithfulness. They believe that God promises always to heal. Since healing is in the Atonement, our prayers for the sick should be answered affirmatively and immediately. When we choose to believe that God is healing us, then God should heal us. There should be no delays and there certainly should be no emphasis on mystery. In fact, one faith preacher sent an e-mail to me in which he made the comment that 'healing and miracles are not sovereign acts of God and therefore mysterious *in the way that some think*'.

While John Wimber emphasized divine sovereignty and God's freedom, the faith preachers have chosen to emphasize God's faithfulness. My personal view is that we should not only distinguish between God's freedom and his faithfulness but also between God's secret and his revealed will (Deut. 29:29). He has not chosen to reveal that he will heal every sick person that is prayed for in faith. Rather, I need to discover the 'secret' will of God for every sick person. Sometimes this will mean preparing them for heaven rather than emphasizing healing alone.

A general list of all the contrasts between these two models follows:

Two models of healing prayer		
	Kingdom model	**Faith model**
Type	Confrontational	Soeteriological
Tradition	Charistmatic/Third Wave	Pentecostal/First Wave
Theology	Calvinist/ Reformed	Arminian
Attribute of God stressed	God's freedom	God's faithfulness
Initiative in healing process	God	Us
Prayer	'Your kingdom come'	'This belongs to me because of what Jesus has done'
Focus	Kingdom of God	The Cross
Doctrine of last things	Now and not yet	Now
Answer to why some are not healed	Mystery of kingdom: it is 'not yet' as well as now	Lack of faith in person receiving prayer or in the person praying

Chapter 5

God's Will and Our Faith

MARK STIBBE

The *Collins English Dictionary* defines the word 'paradox' as 'a person or a thing exhibiting apparently contradictory characteristics'. Anyone who engages seriously in the ministry of divine healing sooner or later has to confront one of the biggest paradoxes of Christianity. I call this the paradox of divine sovereignty and human faith. The truth is there are some who stress that all healing is the result of God sovereignly deciding who gets healed and when. In this model it is supremely and uniquely God who takes the initiative in the healing process. At the same time there are others who stress that healing is the result of us believing that God will heal. In this model it is we who take the initiative in the healing process, coming to God believing that healing is promised to all those who truly believe.

Of course, this paradox of divine sovereignty and human faith applies to a lot of other areas besides healing. In the matter of salvation the same paradox applies. There are some who stress that it is God who takes the initiative when a person comes to Christ and is born again. The whole process is initiated by God the Father, who draws people to himself through his Son and by the power of the Holy Spirit. At the same time, there are others who say that it is we, not God, who take the initiative. It is we who choose to give our lives to the Lord Jesus Christ, to turn from our sins and to enter into the abundant life that Jesus has won for us at the Cross. Some stress divine sovereignty in the matter of salvation. Others stress human believing.

There is no doubt that we are travelling in very deep and often murky waters here. Divine healing really does seem to be a paradox – 'a thing exhibiting apparently contradictory characteristics'. When we are confronted by such difficult questions, we need to go back to the person of Jesus and see what we can learn from his ministry and his message. What does the healing ministry of Jesus suggest about the relationship between God's will and our faith in the matter of divine healing?

When Jesus takes the initiative

There is a story in the Gospels that is often used by those who want to illustrate the way in which God takes the initiative in the matter of divine healing. This passage is in John chapter 5 and occurs at the Pool of Bethesda. For a long time this whole episode was regarded as fictional because no such pool had ever been discovered in Jerusalem. However, archaeologists not long ago discovered the existence of such a healing spa within a short distance of the Temple, and the historical value of the account has been justly reinstated.

The story takes place in Jerusalem at the time of one of the Jewish feasts. Just beyond the entrance of the Sheep Gate there is a pool where many sick people are lying. One of the sick people there is a man who has been paralysed for thirty-eight years. He is singled out among the crowds gathered in that place. All the sick were waiting for the waters to stir in the pool because they believed this was caused by an angel. When the water stirred, the first person into the pool – they thought – would receive healing.

John reports that Jesus set his eyes upon this one man who had been paralysed for thirty-eight years. He also says that Jesus learned that he had been sick for this length of time. It is not made clear whether this was by revelation or the result of asking someone nearby. In any event he focuses his attention on this individual and asks him whether he wants to get well. The man replies that he has no chance of getting well because there is no one to help him into the water when it stirs. Clearly, then, this man has no idea who Jesus is or what Jesus can do for him. Jesus ignores the man's negative response and issues a command: 'Stand up, pick up your mat, and walk!' John reports that the man is instantly healed.

Immediately after this, controversy breaks out. The man is seen walking around with his mat on the Sabbath, which was expressly forbidden at the time. The Jewish leaders see him doing this and ask him why he is breaking Sabbath law. He replies that the man who healed him told him to do this. However, Jesus has disappeared into the crowd so there is no way he can be interrogated.

The story ends with Jesus returning and finding the man in the Temple precincts. Jesus utters a firm warning to the man to stop sinning, otherwise he may experience something far worse than his paralysis. The exact nature of the man's sin is not specified. But clearly Jesus is pointing to a relationship between sin and sickness here. The man, realizing now who Jesus really is, goes off to the religious leaders who had interrogated him and tells them who was responsible for his healing. John does not make it clear whether this was an innocent act or an example of treachery. Whatever the case, the leaders now know who was responsible for telling the man to break the law and from this time on they vow to kill Jesus.

As so often in John's Gospel, a story of Jesus doing something is followed by a passage of Jesus saying something, usually related to the action just performed. This is a case in point. John 5:1–15 describes the healing miracle at the Pool of Bethesda. The rest of the chapter is mostly composed of Jesus teaching in the light of this miracle.

The very first words he utters after the miracle itself are:

> *I assure you, the Son can do nothing by himself. He does only what he sees the Father doing. Whatever the Father does, the Son also does. For the Father loves the Son and tells him everything he is doing, and the Son will do far greater things than healing this man. You will be astonished at what he does. He will even raise from the dead anyone he wants to, just as the Father does (Jn. 5:19–21).*

If one thing comes through loud and clear from these words, it is the extraordinarily intimate communion between Jesus and his Father. Here Jesus expresses his utter dependence upon the Father. He only ever does what he sees his Father doing.

This exceptional, indeed unique, intimacy with the Father is the source of every word and act in Jesus' ministry. This of course includes the healing miracles of Jesus. Indeed, the words in John 5:19 function as a commentary on the healing miracle that has just happened at the Pool of Bethesda. There is no doubt that the healing happens because Jesus feels directed by the Father to heal this specific person. As soon as we realize this, we quite naturally feel a strange mixture of both wonder and curiosity: wonder that the Father should choose a person for such a dramatic restoration to health; curiosity that the Father should single out one man in a crowd of many sick people.

This is where the episode proves so foundational for those who believe that divine healing is the result of God's initiative rather than our own. Those who stress the sovereignty of God in the healing ministry find this episode insightful. Jesus Christ is the exact representation of the Father. To know God, you only have to look at Jesus. Indeed, the person who has seen Jesus has seen the Father. If Jesus only heals one man among many, this shows that it is not always God's will to heal every single sick person right now. He is totally sovereign in the matter of divine healing. He chooses who gets healed and when. The important thing for those who pray for divine healing is to be like Jesus. We must listen to what the Father is saying and depend upon that revelation as we proceed with healing prayer. As we track what the Father is saying and doing, we respond to his initiative and follow his lead. As has often been pointed out, this means blessing what God is doing rather than asking God to bless what we are doing.

The problem with this particular model is the fact that those who are not healed may develop an image of God as a somewhat capricious Father. They may say, 'He has chosen some to get healed, yes, but not me.' While a generous soul may want to celebrate God's goodness to those who have been healed, another person may find doubts beginning to emerge in their own heart about God's goodness to them personally.

When human beings take the initiative

It is at least in part because of this danger that some practitioners in divine healing take an alternative, indeed opposing, viewpoint. Instead of saying that God supernaturally selects a few to be healed, they argue that there are other Gospel episodes (far more in fact) that depict sick people taking the initiative in the healing process.

Perhaps pre-eminent among all such passages is the story told by Mark in chapter 5 of his Gospel. Just to set the scene, the story in question occurs in a series of episodes that are designed to illustrate Jesus' supremacy over all the works of the enemy – dangers, demons, disease and death. In the first scene, Jesus is in a boat crossing the Sea of Galilee in a great storm (Mk. 4:35–41). That this storm has been stirred up by the devil is clearly demonstrated by the way Jesus deals with it. He issues the same kind of rebuke to the wind and the waves as he does to the demons elsewhere in the Gospel.

In the next scene, Jesus has crossed from the Jewish to the Gentile or pagan side of the lake. He is now confronted by a man with a legion of demons (Mk. 5:1–20). Jesus successfully delivers this poor man from his terrible affliction and he then leaves this territory. Clearly, Jesus is seen to be Lord of both Jewish and Gentile sides of the lake in this dramatic episode.

Jesus' authority is further emphasized in Mark 5:21–43, where we get one of Mark's famous 'sandwich effects'. This involves Mark putting three sections of narrative together, the outer two having to do with the same subject, and the inner one (the 'meat', as it were) dealing with some related subject. In this instance, the 'pieces of bread' deal with Jesus being summoned to raise a dead girl to life. Verses 21–24 and 35–43 deal with the raising of Jairus's twelve-year-old daughter from death. It is a touching and powerful scene.

In the middle of these two sections (verses 25–34) lies the story that we are focusing on, a remarkable healing miracle. As Jesus walks to Jairus's house, crowds throng around him. Mark then reports:

*And there was a woman in the crowd who had had a haemorrhage
for twelve years. She had suffered a great deal from many doctors
through the years and had spent everything she had to pay them, but
she had got no better. In fact, she was worse. She had heard about
Jesus, so she came up behind him through the crowd and touched
the fringe of his robe. For she thought to herself, 'If I can just touch
his clothing, I will be healed.' Immediately the bleeding stopped, and
she could feel that she had been healed! (Mk. 5:25–30).*

Here a woman who has been suffering from an appalling
bleeding disorder for twelve years approaches Jesus from
behind. She is absolutely desperate to be made well,
having suffered unsuccessful treatment from the medics
of her day. She truly believes, however, that Jesus is no
ordinary man. Something inside her heart says, 'If only
I reach out and touch his prayer shawl, I will be healed.'
Now that is faith. This woman believes in Jesus' power to
heal in spite of her dire circumstances. With faith in her
heart, she reaches out and touches Jesus, and Mark says
'immediately' (one of his favourite words) the bleeding
stopped and she could actually feel she was restored to
full health.

What happens next is very revealing:

*Jesus realized at once that healing power had gone out from him,
so he turned around in the crowd and asked, 'Who touched my
clothes?' His disciples said to him, 'All this crowd is pressing
around you. How can you ask, "Who touched me?"' But he kept
on looking around to see who had done it. Then the frightened
woman, trembling at the realization of what had happened to her,
came and fell at his feet and told him what she had done. And he
said to her, 'Daughter, your faith has made you well. Go in peace.
You have been healed' (Mk. 5:30–34).*

If ever there was an episode in the Gospels that seems to
illustrate that human beings take the initiative in divine

healing, it has to be this one. Jesus seems surprised that someone has touched him. He does not seem to know who it is either. He asks people around him who was responsible and his disciples tell him that there are so many that it is impossible to tell. Jesus keeps looking around until the woman eventually plucks up courage to come and tell him that it was her. Jesus' words to her are immensely significant. He does not say, 'I have healed you.' He says, 'Your faith has made you well.' He then dismisses her with words of 'shalom' and reassures her that she has now been healed.

We can see now why this episode is so foundational for those who believe that divine healing is the result of our faith more than God's sovereign activity. Those who stress the human side of the equation find this episode insightful because it shows the woman clearly taking the initiative, not Jesus. She is the active one in the healing process, not Jesus. Jesus does not utter a word or perform any actions until after the woman has touched him and healing power has gone out from him. It is her faith that counts here. Anyone who argues otherwise is clearly contradicting Jesus' own words when he stresses that it was her faith that healed her.

For this reason there are many who choose to stress the role of our believing in the process of divine healing. For them it is our faith that is the really critical thing. What the sick need to do is to believe without doubt in God's will to heal. They need to come to Jesus asking in faith for what they know he has the power to do. This of course is the very opposite end of the spectrum to the one mentioned earlier. While the first model puts the emphasis on what God does, this one puts the emphasis on what we do. It involves placing the focus much more on the person who wants healing, urging them to believe that their healing is made possible because of what Jesus has done on the Cross, encouraging them to understand that their Heavenly Father wants them to be made well. If the first model stresses the divine side of the healing process, the second one stresses the human side.

The problem with this model is of course the simple fact that experience does not match up to the theology. Even the most earnest and sincere proponents of this kind of approach admit that there are people who do not get healed. Even when faith levels are at their highest, and people clearly are receiving a measure of healing, there is nearly always someone left unhealed. What happens in their situation? To be sure, they may be encouraged to come and ask again. But the danger inherent in the faith model is that eventually the sick person will come to the inevitable conclusion that they have not been healed because they lack sufficient faith. Now they are in a worse situation than before they came for prayer. If it was bad enough that they were ill, now they have to contend with the additional guilt of not having enough faith for their healing.

An old debate revived

It is important for us to understand that this discussion is not by any means new. Ever since the earliest days of the church, theologians have been trying to understand the relationship between God's sovereign will and our faith. The debate raged particularly fiercely in the time of the Reformation during the sixteenth century. It revolved around two great theologians, Swiss pastor John Calvin (1509–64) and Dutch minister Jacob Arminius (1560–1609).

It is helpful to begin with Arminius' views first. After Arminius' death in 1609, forty-five of his followers reduced the whole of Arminian theology to five key points.

First, Arminius believed that the Fall had not rendered human beings completely helpless. To be sure, the Fall radically affected and indeed *infected* humanity. Yet, at the same time, fallen human beings have free will and are able to choose whether or not to accept the offer of grace given through Jesus. Every sinner therefore has the freedom to receive or resist the free gift of God in Christ Jesus. God does not make us say either 'yes' or 'no' to him. He respects our freedom to choose and leaves the decision to us.

Secondly, Arminius argued that God foreknew who would receive or resist salvation. However, instead of saying that God had preordained who would decide for and against him, Arminius said that God saw in advance which of us would freely choose to accept or reject the Gospel. In Arminius' view, the sinner chooses Christ. Christ does not choose the sinner. Election is therefore wholly conditional. Being chosen by God is conditional upon our decision to believe the Good News.

Thirdly, Arminius believed that what Jesus achieved on the Cross was for absolutely everyone. Put more technically, Arminius believed in a 'Universal Atonement'. The atonement is available to all but effective only for those who freely choose to receive its benefits.

Fourthly, Arminius believed that the Holy Spirit challenges every person who hears the Gospel message. While outwardly the Gospel is being shared, inwardly the hearer is being called by the Holy Spirit to respond. However, this does not mean that the person hearing the Gospel will find the work of the Spirit irresistible. The sinner can say no to what the preacher is saying and the Holy Spirit is urging. Grace is not irresistible.

Finally, Arminius argued that those who do say yes to the offer of salvation will lose that salvation if they fall from grace. Though some Arminianists disagree that Arminius taught this, many feel that it is a fair representation of what Arminius taught. Arminius did not believe that we are 'once saved, always saved'. We can lose our salvation if we fall away.

The five main points of Calvin's theology directly oppose these five main points of what is called 'Arminianism'. The main tenets of Calvinism can be found in John Calvin's classic work *Institutes of the Christian Religion*. The five key points have been reduced to an acrostic using the word 'TULIP':

T   Total depravity
U   Unconditional election
L   Limited atonement
I   Irresistible grace
P   Perseverance of the saints

Calvin first of all argued that human beings are totally depraved. While Arminius said that human beings are fallen yet still able to choose grace, Calvin argued that the Fall had rendered human beings totally incapable of responding to God. In Arminius' system, we can freely choose to respond in faith to the Gospel. Faith is our gift to God. But in Calvin's system the opposite is true. Faith is not something we contribute to salvation but is itself a part of God's gift of salvation – it is God's gift to the sinner, not the sinner's gift to God. In and of ourselves, we are simply too depraved to choose to believe.

Calvin secondly argued for 'unconditional election'. What does that mean? While Arminius taught that the sinner chooses Christ, Calvin argued that Christ chooses the sinner. In Calvin's thinking, God has chosen certain people to respond to him from before the foundation of the world. This election is completely unconditional. It is based not on what we do but on what God does. In short, it rests solely on his sovereign will. God therefore does not foresee who will freely choose to repent and believe.

Rather, he selects those to whom he will grant the gifts of repentance and faith. God's choice of the sinner, not the sinner's choice of God, is the ultimate cause of salvation.

Calvin thirdly believed in 'limited atonement'. While Arminius argued that the atonement was for everyone, Calvin believed that the atonement was only effective for those whom God had already chosen.

Fourthly, Calvin believed in 'irresistible grace'. Those chosen by God will find his grace irresistible when they hear the Gospel. The internal call of the Holy Spirit cannot be rejected by one who has been chosen. The work of the Spirit is not dependent upon human cooperation. The Spirit's work of causing the chosen to repent and believe is quite simply invincible.

Finally, Calvin argued that those who are truly chosen will not fall away from the faith. The elect will be given the grace to endure. By the power of Almighty God, the elect are kept in faith and are enabled by the Holy Spirit to endure to the end. The 'perseverance of the saints' is accordingly part of the gift of salvation to those whom God chose in advance.

Two opposing views of salvation

It may be helpful to summarize the principal differences between Arminianism and Calvinism using a simple chart:

Theology	Calvinism	Arminianism
Original sin	Total depravity; people cannot respond to God because of sin	Infected by the Fall but not totally helpless

Theology	Calvinism	Arminianism
Human will	Captive to sin	Free to choose good over evil
Grace of God	Saving grace is extended only to the elect	Saving grace is extended to all those who choose to believe
Predestination	God decides in advance who will be saved	God sees in advance who will freely choose salvation
Regeneration	God's work alone	Cooperation of God and human efforts
Extent of the atonement	Limited to the elect	Unlimited and intended for all
Application of the atonement	God enables the elect to respond to the Gospel by his Spirit	Human beings freely choose to respond to the Gospel
Order of salvation	God chooses who will be saved; he calls to them, gives them faith, enables them to repent and be born again, etc.	God calls out to sinners; they feeely choose to respond in repentance and faith, then receive rebirth by the Spirit, etc.
Perseverance	God enables the elect to persevere to the end	Perseverance to the end is dependent on our obedience

So what is the essential difference between these two ways of thinking? In the Arminian way, salvation is the result of the combined efforts of both God and human beings. God takes the initiative in providing the free offer of salvation through what Jesus has done on the Cross. This provision becomes effective when human beings freely choose to cooperate with him and accept the offer of salvation. The critical factor is therefore not God's decision but our free will. God does not cause us to be saved. We choose as an act of the will to say yes. It is therefore we who determine the outcome, not God.

In Calvinism, the opposite is true. Salvation is wholly the result of God's work, not ours. Salvation in Calvin's thinking is the work of the Triune God. God the Father chooses who will be saved before the foundation of the world. God the Son dies on the Cross for those already chosen for salvation. The Holy Spirit works internally in the lives of the chosen to draw them irresistibly into God's love, causing them to respond to the Gospel. In this theology, it is God, not us, who determines who is saved and who is not.

All this has massive implications for our attitude towards evangelism, towards witnessing to non-Christians about Jesus. Whichever theology is your template – Calvinism or Arminianism – it will radically affect your attitude to sharing the Gospel.

Let's begin with Calvinism. On one side of the chart below you will see the positive effects of Calvinism for evangelism. On the other you will see the potential drawbacks.

Positive	Negative
The fact that God has chosen certain people in advance for salvation means that I will be fruitful in evangelism. I can persevere in confidence, knowing that I will sooner or later witness to someone who will find the Gospel irresistible.	If God has predetermined who will be saved and who will be condemned (sometimes known as the doctrine of 'double' predestination), why bother evangelizing at all? God has already decided, so he doesn't need our help.

There is no doubt that Calvinism could very well have both positive and negative effects in evangelism. Positively, it will motivate us to know that some will find God's salvation an offer they simply cannot refuse. This will enable us to persevere when people say no. On the other hand, the danger of an extreme form of Calvinism is that it may encourage passivity in sharing one's faith. This was what lay behind the thinking of those who opposed William Carey's missionary work to India. They said, 'Sit down, young man! If God wants to save the people in India, he can well do so without your help. '

Are things any better if Arminianism is our 'default' position theologically? Here again there are positive and negative consequences for evangelism:

Positive	Negative
We are motivated to share our faith with non-Christians because we know that everyone can	Evangelism puts far too heavy a responsibility upon my shoulders. If every person's salvation

freely choose whether to say yes or no to the offer of salvation. In the Arminian framework, God has not decided in advance who will freely say yes and no. He has simply foreseen that outcome. This means that evangelism is a great responsibility.	is dependent upon my witness, this is far too weighty a burden. Surely God has some role in the process? Surely the lost have some responsibility too? The downside of Arminianism is that it leads me into taking on more responsibility for people's salvation than is rightfully mine.

Again, there is little doubt that Arminianism could well have both positive and negative effects in evangelism. On the plus side, knowing that every unbeliever can freely choose to say yes or no to the Gospel motivates me to evangelize as many people as possible. This lay behind the thinking of John Wesley, the principal evangelist of the eighteenth-century revival in Great Britain. On the minus side, if human free will is the deciding factor, I may start to indulge in the opposite of passivity. I may start to evangelize in my own strength, forgetting that it is not by human might, not by human strength, but by God's Spirit that miracles occur (Zech. 4:6).

What is clear from this brief summary is that what you believe radically determines how you behave. If Calvinism is your default perspective, it will affect the way you evangelize. If Arminianism is your default perspective, this, too, will have a major effect on whether you share your faith with others, and indeed how. Many Christians are probably unaware of the extent to which these two theologies of salvation have formed a template for their thinking and conduct. However, we must become more aware of what we believe, and we must dare to explore and refine our beliefs where necessary. As we shall see, this is especially important in the matter of divine healing.

How belief affects behaviour

What we believe about these issues affects how we interpret what the Bible has to say about divine healing. Let's take the two episodes mentioned earlier in this chapter as test cases.

The first story we looked at was John 5:1–18, the episode in which Jesus singles out a man paralysed for thirty-eight years in a crowd of people. Now a Calvinist would understand this incident as an example of the sovereignty of God. Jesus only did what the Father was doing. The Father had decreed that this one man should be selected out of everyone present for healing. There was nothing in this man that meant that he merited this healing. Like everyone else at the pool, he was a sinner. But Jesus chose the paralysed man. The paralysed man did not choose Jesus. Jesus healed this one person and extended that healing to him alone as the Father's gift. This healing was 'limited' in extent, in that it was only given to one man. In spite of his faults, that one man found the offer of grace 'irresistible'. Further, he was given clear instructions regarding how to persevere in his healing and not to lose the newfound health he had been given. 'Don't sin any more or something worse will happen to you.'

An Arminian coming to this text would see it in a wholly different light. From an Arminian perspective, the offer of healing in this episode was not limited. All the people in the area of the Pool of Bethesda could have responded to the offer of healing. To be sure, Jesus singles out one person, but had the others come to Jesus they would not have been refused their healing. Everywhere else in the Gospels, Jesus heals everyone who comes to him asking for healing, no matter what their disease or disability. Here the same would have applied. Had all the others approached Jesus, he would have extended the same gift to them as he did to the paralysed man. Then all it would have required for them to be healed is for them to say what the paralysed man said: 'I am willing.' In other words, 'I say yes to the offer of healing as an act of free choice.'

The second episode we looked at also involved Jesus and a crowd. In this story, recorded in Mark chapter 5, a woman who has been suffering from a bleeding disorder for twelve years pushes through the crowds and touches Jesus. Power goes out from him and she is instantly healed. When Jesus finds out who it was, he announces that it was her faith that healed her.

For an Arminian, this passage would provide a classic example of the importance of faith. Jesus did not choose the woman: the woman chose Jesus. Jesus did not take the initiative to select just one person among many to receive healing. She chose to take the initiative and come to Jesus in desperation. Even though she was a sinner, and indeed ceremonially 'unclean' because of her affliction, she had enough faith and goodness even in her fallen state to come to Jesus and receive what she so desperately needed. This, the Arminian would argue, is a picture of how it is for all who seek healing. Healing happens when people have enough faith to come to Jesus and touch the hem of his garment. The emphasis of the whole story is on the woman's faith. It is her faith that secures her healing, not the initiative of Jesus.

From a Calvinistic perspective, the passage would be understood in a different light. Certainly the emphasis here is on faith, but this does not mean that God did not predetermine this woman's healing. Does Jesus not say that no one comes to the Father unless the Father 'draws' them (Jn. 6:44)? If that is so, this woman may look as though she is taking the initiative in receiving her healing but in reality it is the Father who takes the leading role. He is the one who draws her to the place and the person where she can find what she so earnestly seeks. It is his Holy Spirit whose grace she finds so irresistible in her life. Even the faith that she so obviously demonstrates is a gift from God. More than that, she is the only person healed within that particular crowd. There must have been others who were sick and in need as well. But Mark records only one finding healing from Jesus. The gift was accordingly limited, not unlimited.

We can see already from these examples that what we believe affects our behaviour when it comes to divine healing. Those who have a Calvinistic template will give priority to the leading of the Holy Spirit. In other words, Calvinists – providing they haven't fallen for the view that miracles ceased at the end of the first century – will start by asking the Father what he is doing in the sick person's life. In practice, this means the person ministering divine healing will spend time listening to God, asking, 'Father, what are you saying? What are you doing?' The ability to hear the Father's voice will determine everything that subsequently occurs. To be sure, faith will be an important ingredient, but faith understood as a gift of God, not as something mustered up by us.

Those who have an Arminian template will use a different approach. The offer of healing is unlimited, not limited. It is not dependent upon God's selection but upon people's faith. Therefore, the Arminian method of praying for the sick is much more likely to stress the importance of coming to Jesus with simple faith in his power to heal. No emphasis will be placed on watching what the Holy Spirit is doing, or on gifts of the Spirit like prophecy. Rather, the person receiving prayer will be encouraged to believe that their healing is available to them right now by faith. In this model, the sick person is much more likely to be asked to demonstrate their faith by walking out of their wheelchair or by some similar action. On receiving any healing, the person will be urged to keep their healing by continuing to walk by faith.

The radical middle

By now many readers may well be wondering which of these two theological frameworks is right. Both of them have persuasive aspects and both have produced spiritual giants. Jonathan Edwards adopted a Calvinistic theology and was greatly used by God in bringing many people to Christ during the revival in North America in the eighteenth century. Charles Finney, who had a more Arminian theology, was similarly greatly used in evangelism in the awakening in North America in the 1820s and 1830s.

The same is true in relation to divine healing. I have witnessed preachers of a Calvinistic persuasion being used mightily by God for the healing of the sick. But the same is also true of preachers with a more Arminian worldview. I have seen God use people coming from entirely opposing camps in divine healing. Truly, the work of the Holy Spirit can sometimes be more elusive than our tidy theologies permit!

In another book I co-authored, also published by Authentic, I looked at the Steven Spielberg film *Minority Report*. This film is about the degree to which our futures are predetermined, and the degree to which we choose to create our futures. The book was called *The Big Picture 2*, and the chapter was entitled 'Is my Future Fixed?' In preparing that chapter I came across a great quote from the nineteenth-century Baptist preacher Charles Spurgeon. He also grappled with the issues of Calvinistic and Arminian theology and said:

> When a Calvinist says that all things happen according to the predestination of God, he speaks the truth, and I am willing to be called a Calvinist. But when an Arminian says that when a man sins, the sin is his own, and that if he continues in sin, and perishes, his eternal damnation will lie entirely at his own door, I believe that he speaks the truth, though I am not willing to be called an Arminian. The fact is, there is some truth in both these systems of theology.

A similar reasoning can be applied to the matter of divine healing. When a Calvinist says that all healing miracles occur because God has decreed they should, I am willing to be called a Calvinist. But when an Arminian says that our faith is critical for securing divine healing, and that we have to play an active part in the healing process, I am convinced that he or she speaks the truth – though, like Spurgeon, I am not willing to be called an Arminian. The fact is, there is some truth in both these systems of theology, at least when it comes to divine healing.

In the final analysis, I believe we must do two things. We must first of all allow God to be God and follow the leading of his Holy Spirit as we pray for healing. At the same time, we need to exercise faith. The Bible teaches that there is a war on and that we need to fight the good fight. We therefore need to believe – and go on believing – for what we cannot yet see. The 'radical middle' that I want to suggest therefore implies two things: first, God's will is paramount; secondly, we need to grow in faith and exercise that faith in a prevailing and persistent way with those who need healing prayer.

Perhaps, in conclusion, Smith Wigglesworth's example is instructive here. It is hard to think of anyone who saw more dramatic healing miracles in the UK in the twentieth century than Smith Wigglesworth. Indeed, so great was Smith's faith that he has been called 'the Apostle of faith'. He challenged everyone involved in the healing ministry to grow in faith. As Julian Wilson reports in his biography, *Wigglesworth: The Complete Story*:

> When out for a walk with some young men from a church, he was asked how one could possess great faith. His reply was as typically laconic as it was profound: 'First the blade, then the ear; then the full corn in the ear,' he said, quoting from Mark 4:28. 'Faith must grow by soil, moisture and exercise.'

On the one hand, Smith Wigglesworth exercised great faith when he prayed for divine healing. On the other hand, he always began with asking God what he wanted to do. As Julian Wilson puts it, 'His method of praying for people always depended, according to Wigglesworth, on "what the Father had to say".' This dependency on God's will meant that Wigglesworth had room for mystery as well as miracle in his theology. Sometimes people were not healed when he prayed for them. His daughter Alice was never healed of deafness in spite of her father praying for her many times. Smith himself experienced illness and disability. In his fifties he began wearing glasses because his sight deteriorated. This led Smith to the conclusion that 'he who can explain divine healing can explain God'.

Smith Wigglesworth's example is not a bad one to follow. He believed passionately that God's will is paramount and that the important thing was to do what the Father wanted to do. This meant that sometimes people were not healed, something that is impossible to explain fully. At the same time, he exercised tremendous faith and encouraged, cajoled and even chastised others to do the same, urging people to be desperate for their healing and to pray for the sick with the unshakeable conviction that nothing is too hard for the Lord.

Perhaps this is the best place, in the end, to situate ourselves theologically. This is the 'radical middle' between the overly Calvinistic and the overly Arminian approaches to divine healing. In this 'radical middle' we accept fully the precious and indispensable doctrine of God's sovereignty, understanding that divine healing is the result of God's free but not his necessary will. At the same time, we hear clearly the biblical call to engage in spiritual warfare, praying for the sick and the oppressed (the casualties of war, as it were), and believing in God's mighty power to do supernatural wonders that are beyond what medicine can achieve and science can explain. This may not be a final solution to the great complexities we have touched on in this chapter, but it is a biblical and a practical one. It creates a space in which we can see a creative fusion between God's initiative and ours – a space in which the power of the Spirit is released for the healing of the sick, to the glory and honour of the name of Jesus.

Part 2

MINISTERING DIVINE HEALING

Chapter 6

Creating a Healing Community

MARK STIBBE

I remember speaking at a conference where the other guest speaker was Pentecostal scholar Professor Gordon Fee. We were sharing a day of teaching on the Holy Spirit. I will never forget Gordon sharing his insights about the differences between churches today and churches in the New Testament era. He made the startling and challenging point that the biggest difference in today's churches was the lack of what he called 'the empowering presence of God'. He argued that if the Apostle Paul were alive today and went on a journey visiting local churches in contemporary Britain, the biggest thing that would strike and disturb him would be the lack of any visible signs of the manifest presence of God.

This is a challenging thought. David Parker, currently senior pastor of the Desert Vineyard Church in Lancaster, California, was at one time on staff at St Andrew's Chorleywood. As an American in Britain he had to get used to our underground system in London. On one occasion he heard an instruction repeated several times over the public address system. It simply said, 'Mind the gap. Mind the gap.' As he heard this, David sensed the Holy Spirit saying that he was to tell the churches in the UK to 'mind the gap'. In other words, we are to give prayerful and serious attention to the gap between what the churches were like in the New Testament and what the churches are like today. David spent the following two years visiting churches throughout the UK, trying to impress upon them the need to 'mind the gap'.

Minding the gap

A cursory reading of the pages of the New Testament reveals the gap between local churches then and many local churches now. One thing is particularly noticeable: the New Testament churches for the most part lived in an atmosphere of the miraculous. Even a casual examination of the evidence shows that this was widespread in the earliest churches.

The believers in Jerusalem

A deep sense of awe came over them all, and the apostles performed many miraculous signs and wonders (Acts 2:43).

But Peter said, 'I don't have any money for you. But I'll give you what I have. In the name of Jesus Christ of Nazareth, get up and walk!' (Acts 3:6).

As a result of the apostles' work, sick people were brought out into the streets on beds and mats so that Peter's shadow might fall across some of them as he went by. Crowds came in from the villages around Jerusalem, bringing their sick and those possessed by evil spirits, and they were all healed (Acts 5:15–16).

The believers in Samaria

Philip ... went to the city of Samaria and told the people there about the Messiah. Crowds listened intently to what he had to say because of the miracles he did. Many evil spirits were cast out, screaming as they left their victims. And many who had been paralysed or lame were healed (Acts 8:5–8).

The believers in Lydda

Peter travelled from place to place to visit the believers, and in his travels he came to the Lord's people in the town of Lydda. There he met a man named Aeneas, who had been paralysed and bedridden for eight years. Peter said to him, 'Aeneas, Jesus Christ heals you! Get up and make your bed!' And he was healed instantly. Then the whole population of Lydda and Sharon turned to the Lord when they saw Aeneas walking around (Acts 9:32–35).

The believers in Joppa

But Peter asked them all to leave the room; then he knelt and prayed. Turning to the body he said, 'Get up, Tabitha.' And she opened her eyes! When she saw Peter, she sat up! (Acts 9:40).

The believers in Antioch

The power of the Lord was upon them, and large numbers of these Gentiles believed and turned to the Lord (Acts 11:21).

The believers in Iconium

The apostles stayed there a long time, preaching boldly about the grace of the Lord. The Lord proved their message was true by giving them power to do miraculous signs and wonders (Acts 14:3).

The believers in Lystra

While they were at Lystra, Paul and Barnabas came upon a man with crippled feet. He had been that way from birth, so he had never walked. He was listening as Paul preached, and Paul noticed him and realized he had faith to be healed. So Paul called to him in a loud voice, 'Stand up!' And the man jumped to his feet and started walking (Acts 14:8–10)

The believers in Philippi

This went on day after day until Paul got so exasperated that he turned and spoke to the demon within her. 'I command you in the name of Jesus Christ to come out of her,' he said. And instantly it left her (Acts 16:18).

The believers in Ephesus

God gave Paul the power to do unusual miracles, so that even when handkerchiefs or cloths that had touched his skin were placed on sick people, they were healed of their diseases, and any evil spirits within them came out (Acts 19:11–12).

The believers in Troas

As Paul spoke on and on, a young man named Eutychus, sitting on the windowsill, became very drowsy. Finally, he sank into a deep sleep and fell three stories to his death below. Paul went down, bent over him, and took him into his arms. 'Don't worry,' he said, 'he's alive!' (Acts 20:9–10).

Reading through the Book of Acts, it is clear that the earliest churches experienced all kinds of miracles. They witnessed resurrection miracles, miracles of judgment (such as the death of Ananias and Sapphira in Acts 5), prison release miracles (such as Peter's great escape in Acts 12), deliverance miracles or 'exorcisms', 'extraordinary miracles' (involving handkerchiefs and aprons, as in Acts 19), and most commonly healing miracles. As Professor James Dunn observes in his classic book *Jesus and the Spirit*,

'There was a power to heal present in these first Christian communities, and a numinous power too which seems to have caused as much fear as it did popularity.'

And this fact is not just recorded in the narrative portions of the New Testament (such as the Book of Acts). It is reflected in the letters of the New Testament as well. So Paul, reflecting on his missionary work among the Gentiles, says in Romans 15:19:

> *I have won them over by the miracles done through me as signs from God – all by the power of God's Spirit. In this way, I have fully presented the Good News of Christ all the way from Jerusalem right over into Illyricum.*

In Paul's letters to the Corinthians there are references to miracles. In 1 Corinthians 4:20 he reminds his readers that 'the Kingdom of God is not just fancy talk; it is living by God's power'. In 2 Corinthians 12:12 he writes:

> *When I was with you, I certainly gave you every proof that I am truly an apostle, sent to you by God himself. For I patiently did many signs and wonders and miracles among you.*

Writing to the Galatians, Paul asks:

> *Does God give you the Holy Spirit and work miracles among you because you obey the law of Moses? Of course not! It is because you believe the message you heard about Christ (Gal. 3:5).*

These references to miracles are not restricted to Paul's letters either. In the letter to the Hebrews, we are reminded by the writer that 'God verified the message by signs and wonders and various miracles and by giving gifts of the Holy Spirit whenever he chose to do so' (Heb. 2:4). In his letter, the Apostle James writes in 5:14–15:

> *Are any among you sick? They should call for the elders of the*
> *church and have them pray over them, anointing them with oil*
> *in the name of the Lord. And their prayer offered in faith will heal*
> *the sick, and the Lord will make them well. And anyone who has*
> *committed sins will be forgiven.*

Almost everywhere you look in the New Testament, you
see churches experiencing miracles, and particularly
miracles of healing. These happen right across the board
and are attested to in just about every context. Many of
these healing miracles are performed by the apostles. But
some are not (such as those witnessed by Stephen in Acts
6 and Philip in Acts 8). The only places where we do not
find overt references are in the later epistles like Ephesians,
Colossians, and 1 and 2 Timothy. Everywhere else we do.
As Professor James Dunn rightly observes in his book
Jesus and the Spirit:

> We need not doubt that it is a sound historical fact that many
> healings of a miraculous sort did occur in the early days of
> the first Christian communities and of the early Christian
> mission. This is attested at first hand by Paul (Rom. 15.19; 1
> Cor. 12.10, 28f; 2 Cor. 12.12; Gal. 3.5), and also by the writer
> to the Hebrews (Heb. 2.4).

A charismatic community

When we look at the earliest churches we become mindful
of the gap that exists between the experience of the Spirit
now and the experience of the Spirit then. We can take
one of three views on this. We can take the liberal position
that denies that anything miraculous occurred in the New
Testament era, because miracles do not happen. I call
this the 'no then, no now' perspective. We can take the
cessationist position that says that miracles happened in the
New Testament era but they 'ceased' (hence 'cessationism')

at the end of the apostolic age. I call this the 'yes then, no now' perspective. We can finally take a third position, the perspective of the Pentecostals and Charismatics, which argues that miracles occurred in the New Testament churches and they are supposed to occur in today's churches too. I call this the 'yes then, yes now' perspective. It is the third perspective that Marc A. Dupont and I share and are promoting in this book. Both of us believe from our study of the Word and our experience of the Holy Spirit that God healed the sick miraculously through believers in the first century, and that he is still doing the same through believers in the twenty-first century.

When you look carefully at the local churches of the New Testament, you cannot avoid the fact that being a Christian in that era meant being a 'charismatic'. In other words, it meant experiencing God's amazing grace through the power of the Spirit. It meant receiving and ministering in the gifts of the Spirit, the manifestations of God's empowering presence in the local church. Paul describes some of these grace gifts in a list (not exhaustive) in 1 Corinthians 12:8–11:

> *To one person the Spirit gives the ability to give wise advice; to another he gives the gift of special knowledge. The Spirit gives special faith to another, and to someone else he gives the power to heal the sick. He gives one person the power to perform miracles, and to another the ability to prophesy. He gives someone else the ability to know whether it is really the Spirit of God or another spirit that is speaking. Still another person is given the ability to speak in unknown languages, and another is given the ability to interpret what is being said. It is the one and only Holy Spirit who distributes these gifts. He alone decides which gift each person should have.*

I have written a whole book on these verses, entitled *Know Your Spiritual Gifts* (subtitled 'Practising the Presents of

God'), so I will be brief here. In this present context all I want to emphasize is that there were clearly some believers in Paul's day with the special, God-given ability to heal the sick. This ability is not a natural but a supernatural endowment, given because of God's undeserved favour, and administered by the Holy Spirit. Not everyone possessed the gifts of healing. Not everyone was endued with the power to perform miracles. Paul makes this clear in 1 Corinthians 12:29–31:

> *Is everyone an apostle? Of course not. Is everyone a prophet? No. Are all teachers? Does everyone have the power to do miracles? Does everyone have the gift of healing? Of course not. Does God give all of us the ability to speak in unknown languages? Can everyone interpret unknown languages? No! And in any event, you should desire the most helpful gifts.*

Having said that, Paul did expect the local church to be a charismatic community, participating in the life of the Spirit together, experiencing the manifest presence of the Spirit through gifts like healing. As James Dunn writes:

> In 1 Cor. 12.9, 28, 30 we have first hand testimony to the fact that there were cures and healings experienced in the Pauline communities for which no natural or rational explanation would suffice – they could only be put down to the action of God.

Putting all this evidence together we can see very clearly that the local churches of the New Testament era continued to heal the sick and perform miracles, just as Jesus had done. Indeed, Paul's teaching on the church as 'the body of Christ' is critical here. Local churches are the body of Christ. They continue the ministry of Jesus in the world. Believers in a locality are the hands, feet, heart, voice, and so on, of Jesus Christ. They – and we – are supposed to continue doing the work that Jesus did, including healings and miracles. Through us, the risen and ascended Lord continues to heal the sick today, and will continue to do so until he comes again in great glory on the last day. When that day comes, the healing ministry will no longer be needed, because the whole cosmos will have been redeemed and recreated. Until that time, the local church is meant to keep praying for the sick and doing so 'in the name of Jesus'.

Creating a community of healing

Yes, but how? That is the question I sense you asking right now. How do we exercise the healing ministry in the local church today? How can we create a community where there is faith for God to move in the miraculous in people's lives?

In what follows I want to share seven practical suggestions for developing an effective ministry of divine healing in the local church. I am not saying for one moment that this list is either comprehensive or prescriptive. But it is, I believe, biblical and also practical. Indeed, at St Andrew's we try to implement all of these suggestions. We haven't got all the answers, nor do we get everything right. But it may be there are some useful guidelines here for your situation.

Suggestion 1: *Make divine healing a priority*

A local church will never have an ongoing ministry of healing prayer unless this ministry is recognized as one of the core values of the church in question. Offering prayer for divine healing on a regular basis is not an optional

extra for a church; it is part and parcel of God's mission of
salvation to the community in which that church is based,
and beyond that to the ends of the earth. The leadership
of a local church must accordingly give priority to this
ministry and commit to keeping the enthusiasm for it alive
in the congregation through preaching.

In St Andrew's Church there has been a consistent
emphasis on ministering divine healing for a long time.
I would love to take the credit for this but in reality the
initiative began during the time of the first vicar, John
Perry, during the 1960s and 1970s. The second vicar,
Bishop David Pytches, was very influenced by John
Wimber's ministry and, during the 1980s and the early
1990s, established a large prayer ministry team at St
Andrew's which I have had the very great privilege of
inheriting. Today I am under no illusions. The reason
why we have such an amazingly anointed team of people
(about 150-strong) is because my predecessors and their
leadership teams made healing prayer ministry one of the
foundational values and consistent priorities of the church.
I have not had to start a healing ministry team from scratch
(as I did in my last church in Sheffield). I have just had to
keep the fire going.

I would therefore encourage readers who are on the
leadership team of a local church to ensure that prayer
ministry is a core value and that it is offered at every
suitable opportunity in the life of the church. If you are
not on the leadership team of your church you can give a
copy of this book to those who are and encourage them
to consider providing this vital resource.

Suggestion 2: *Provide regular training*

In the back of this book (Appendix) you will find the notes
for our school of ministry. Subjects covered are:

Our acceptance in the Father
Operating in the Spirit's power
Qualities for team members
Prayer ministry and the spiritual gifts
Leading a seeker to Christ
Ministering healing in Jesus' name
How to deliver the oppressed
How to hear the voice of God
The confession of sin
The practice of prayer ministry

At St Andrew's we hold regular training courses. We have an annual course designed to train members in leadership and biblical theology, and this contains intensives on 'Healing and the Kingdom of God'. We hold regular healing ministry training weekends where people can learn how to pray for the sick. and we have a course called, 'The Father Loves You'. This is designed to help people become properly grounded in God's love and to be free from the wounds of their past. All three courses run on Thursday evenings and form the backbone of our Church Training Programme. Anyone who is a member of our church can sign up and come along for this training. However, they do need to have been in a small group for at least six months if they are to enrol in the school of ministry, and they must have the backing of their small group leader, especially if they are to progress from the training course to being involved in praying for others. This is because we believe proper accountability is essential if this ministry is to maintain integrity in the local church.

With the school of ministry, we only really have one opportunity each year to get new people trained, so we make a big plug at the Sunday services and we alert our small group leaders. We do offer another opportunity for our teenagers in another format so they can be trained as well. At the end of the training, I meet with my two ministry team leaders, John and Heather, and we go through the names of those who have been on the course and decide who is to be commissioned and authorized this time, and who needs to wait until later. Just occasionally we have to say no.

When those who have been on the course are ready to start, we give them a white badge and buddy them with an experienced ministry team member (orange badge-holders). This provides a phase of further training with mentoring from the more experienced team member. In addition to all this, several members of our staff take teams of ministry team members out to other churches to help train up prayer ministry teams in other congregations. It is always a joy to give away freely what you have received in this particular area. You can find out details of this ministry on our church web site: www.st-Andrews.org.uk.

One final point regarding training: we deem it very important to have a ministry team feedback meeting every term (three times a year) on a Saturday morning. We do a number of things in this meeting. John and Heather, who oversee this ministry, provide all the information team members need to know, including any necessary comments about good and bad practice. I provide some teaching in an area of prayer ministry that is relevant at the time. Then there is a sharing of testimonies about what the Lord has done through the prayer ministry team over the last term (always very encouraging). Finally, the overseers and a team of musicians spend time praying for and ministering to the team members (which we call 'soaking time').

Suggestion 3: *Provide regular prayer ministry*

Once you have trained a team of people, it is really important to have an organized system for using them both in the main Sunday meetings and at other times. There are five main environments in which we use this ministry. The first is the Sunday services: we offer ministry at the end of each of our three main meetings. We regularly allow space for the Holy Spirit to speak before we move into this ministry. In practice this means devoting the last section of a service to listening to God for words of revelation about people's needs, and then closing the service with a blessing and calling people forward.

A second context in which we provide this ministry is regular healing services. In addition to our ongoing ministry of prayer at every main meeting, we also have regular Sunday evening services, which contain a message and testimonies, etc.

A third context in which we provide this ministry is once a month on a Wednesday morning in our chapel. This again takes the form of a Holy Communion service. It is very informal and ministry team members who don't work and are free come along to help pray for the sick. People come from near and far to receive prayer and we have seen the Lord do wonderful things over the years. The other three Wednesday mornings each month a couple in our church called Robin and Daphne faithfully lead an intercession meeting for those who are sick. Sometimes the sick come to those meetings too and are prayed for.

A fourth context in which we pray for the sick is in a series of healing meetings. Once a year I try to get Marc A. Dupont over from the USA to do a series of a week's meetings (usually culminating in the Sunday services). In those meetings we focus on praying for the sick. We have seen some really significant healings in these week-long missions. We see people who are not Christians giving their lives to Christ, and we also see many people with all kinds of needs gloriously healed and set free. Such weeks, given over exclusively to divine healing, keep faith for healing alive in our church.

A fifth and final context in which we pray for the sick is on our leaders' days and residential conferences. Here again we are very blessed to have a lot of people on our ministry team who are available in the week, because they are either retired or self-employed or not working (for whatever reason). They come to the church and pray for conference delegates with extraordinary compassion and great commitment. As on Sundays and at other times, they always go the extra mile for people, often staying later than anyone, all because they love the Lord and they love praying for those in need.

Suggestion 4: Develop a strategy for follow-up

We stress in our training that the ministry team members are not to engage in what we used to call 'counselling' when people come forward for prayer. Sometimes those who come forward are very wounded and require much more than a few minutes' being prayed for at a service. What they need is a number of sessions with people who are trained to provide inner healing in a more sustained way. Or perhaps they need to come on a 'Father Loves You' course. Or they may need to go on a marriage enrichment course.

Alongside the prayer ministry team it is therefore important to find couples who would be willing and suitable to provide inner healing or what we call 'pastoral prayer ministry'. Again I am very blessed in that my predecessors David and Mary Pytches did a great job getting this resource going in the church. You may not yet be in a position where you have these opportunities or people. But you can pray for God to provide them and work over a period of time to create follow-up systems and strategies for those who need more than just a brief time of prayer on Sundays.

Suggestion 5: Keep sharing people's testimonies

I cannot stress enough the importance of getting ordinary people to tell extraordinary stories of what the Lord has done in their lives. Now obviously we have to be sensitive here because there will be people who have not been healed yet, in spite of much prayer. Whatever happens, the local church needs a theology that has room not only for miracle but also for mystery, as I have said already. At the same time, the fact that some are not healed should never prevent us from praying with great faith for all sick people to be made well. Nor should it prevent us from allowing and encouraging testimonies from those who have clearly received great benefit from healing prayer ministry. Such stories raise faith in God's power to heal, and faith, as we have already seen, is critical in the healing ministry.

One of the most encouraging testimonies we have had recently concerns a woman called Wilma, who came to a couple of healing meetings when Marc A. Dupont was visiting us. In fact, she came to these meetings both in 2003 and in 2004, and on both occasions she received some significant healing. Her story is inspiring and has helped many others to believe for healing in their own lives. Here it is, in her words:

In February 2003 Marc A. Dupont came to St Andrew's to do some healing meetings. At that time I had been progressively ill for twenty years, following a serious operation. My thyroid was underactive and I was very depressed. Then I was told I had ME. In 1996, I resigned from my teaching job as I was simply too exhausted to carry on. I needed to go to bed for a long sleep every afternoon. After a year I was told I had fibromyalgia (that's like ME but with chronic muscular pain). I longed to have the energy again to do all the jobs that seemed to depend on me.

In February last year, I was at the church when Marc was holding a healing meeting. I saw people go forward for healing and watched them shake and fall to the floor. This was definitely not my style. I remarked that 'it all smacked of emotional hysteria'. But, despite this, I was curious.

During the meeting Marc asked everyone to raise their right hand. As I did so, I felt mine had been torched. It was red-hot and full of pins and needles (I suffer from very poor circulation and *cold* hands). Marc then asked everyone who had experienced tingling in their hands to go forward for prayer. I promptly pulled down my hand and stayed put.

In the end I went to the front of the church and two people laid hands on me and asked what needed healing. 'I long not to feel tired,' I said. 'I wake up more tired than I go to bed. I am in constant pain and I am so weary.' As they prayed, I began to weep. When they stopped, I felt as if a huge lead weight had been physically lifted out of my chest and placed elsewhere. I felt remarkably lighter, and unburdened.

That night I slept through without waking for the first time in years – and I awoke feeling refreshed.

The next night, Marc's last, I returned. Every time Marc asked sufferers to come forward, with a pain in their right ear, a bad knee, sore shoulder, backache, I felt they all applied to me. I hurt *everywhere*. So I didn't go up at all. Until I heard the word fibromyalgia. That just *had* to apply to me.

My way was blocked with people suffering from dyslexia, neuralgia and other problems. I finally found myself at the front, right in front of the Cross. And the two people who were sitting on the floor, as if waiting for me to appear, were the two who had prayed for me the previous evening.

The second they placed their hands on my shoulder I fell flat on the floor. I could actually see myself curled up on the carpet. I was about five feet up in the air, looking down on my body. It was making very strange wailing noises. I was quite aware of the situation, that I was totally detached from my body, observing. It was not frightening at all, but it was very vivid. After some time, I was aware of my 'self in the air' being literally drawn back down into my body to be reabsorbed. I thought I should get up. I couldn't. I heard someone say, 'It is the weight of the Holy Spirit'. I thought, 'Yeah, right,' somewhat sceptically.

I was helped into a chair where I tried to make sense of what had happened. There was an enormous sense of 'wholeness' and of well-being. I felt like a 'new person'. I truly felt I had been 'born again' and that I had been given another chance at life. Within a week I had cut out ten of my twelve daily pills. My muscle pain and fatigue had completely gone. I no longer had a daily nap.

I continued only to take the thyroxin, and last week I was told I could stop that if I wanted to as, after twenty years, my thyroid balance is normal.

Last month when Marc A. Dupont returned to St Andrew's I attended his evening talks. On the second night he prayed for the healing of people who had bad knees. I have had five operations on my left knee and need new knees.

That night my knees were prayed for and the next day all pain had gone. Over Easter weekend I walked for three hours up and down extremely steep mountain valleys. Three weeks before this I was unable to walk up three flights of stairs without extreme pain. I suffered no pain at all during our hill climb and I kept saying how miraculous this was.

The third night Marc stopped in his talk and said he had a word about a woman in the church that night who had a problem with her left wrist, 'probably the result of an accident, or arthritis'. He repeated this three times before I felt brave enough to stand up and go forward. Last June I fell off a bike and broke my left wrist very badly. Because I had a flight ahead of me, the doctor could not plaster it so it was splinted for ten days. The break was very bad and the pain dreadful. When the plaster was removed, my wrist looked as if it had been severed then replaced one inch off centre. It looked horribly deformed and was obvious to all. People could not help commenting on it. This past year has been one of pain and weakness in this wrist. I have had osteopathy every three weeks and wear a night splint.

Marc commanded that my wrist be straightened in Jesus' name and that the bones knit. I began to shake uncontrollably. My wrist began to heat up and this heat stayed for about two weeks. Now, after a month, my wrist is almost perfectly straight. I can lift heavy trays, move my hand in all directions. Friends comment on the fact I am using it again, and I get the chance to tell them how God has healed me, yet again!

Apart from the wonderful relief from pain, I am so struck by the fact that the God of the entire universe should know the very last detail of Wilma and her broken wrist. Who am I that he should single me out? I feel like the sparrow in the Bible whose fall God is aware of. I feel so very humbled and blessed. I marvel that he should reach out to me and touch me in this way. It is as if he is saying to me, 'I know you and care about you, even about your left wrist.' This is truly a wonder and a profound joy. It has made me realize that through all my unhappy times when I felt so alone, God was with me and carried me.

These healing experiences have confirmed God's amazing power and love for me. I am overwhelmed and full of joy that he has shown himself to me in this way. I really feel loved and 'born again'. It has changed my life and my outlook for ever and I thank God daily.

People who know me are aware I have changed and they all ask about it. I tell them God healed me and tell them how. Their usual comment is that because I am 'so down to earth' and the last person they would ever expect this to happen to, they have no choice but to believe it.

Testimonies like this are really powerful and we should always give opportunities to share them. When people who are known and loved in the local church receive significant and visible transformation through healing prayer, this needs to be celebrated. We should never allow the focus to fall on the person who has received the prayer or the ones who prayed for the person. Rather we should give thanks to the Lord and always point away from ourselves to Jesus. To put it another way, we should make sure we point away from the healing to the Healer.

Suggestion 6: Keep interceding for the sick

It is very important to use models of healing that are biblical and appropriate for your church. We have chosen to adopt a model of healing that is influenced by John Wimber's teaching. I call this the 'Kingdom model'. But there are other models that are important too. One of these is the 'intercessory model', where on a regular basis the church prays for those who are sick 'by proxy'; i.e. praying for those who are not at the meeting where prayer is being offered. I love the beginning of 3 John where the apostle writes, 'Dear friend, I am praying that all is well with you and that your body is as healthy as I know your soul is' (verse 2). While this is, in a sense, a conventional opening statement for a letter in the ancient world, it is still a great prayer. It is a prayer for an absent friend to experience good health. We should intercede regularly for the sick, praying for wholeness of body, soul and spirit.

We encourage our people to intercede for the sick. This always includes people known to us as a congregation. It also sometimes includes those who are not churchgoers and whom most of us do not know. One example from the last few weeks will have to suffice here. A young man in our twenties group works for a Christian retail company. He has been working with a non-Christian graphic designer called Barry. Barry told him that his baby neice was critically ill in hospital. He vowed to pray for her and to ask others in his small group to pray too. A few days later he received the following from Barry in an e-mail:

> I don't know what you said when you made a prayer for my niece, but since Monday she has taken a remarkable turn. Before the weekend we were basically waiting for her to pass away after being kept alive by machines, and there was no brain activity. Yesterday we heard that she has come off the machines and is now breathing and moving by herself. Although she will have some difficulties, she is past the danger zone, which no doubt the prayer you made must have helped. I told my family that you were sending a prayer and they are very grateful to you, and wanted me to pass on their thanks. If miracles do happen, then I think it definitely happened on this occasion. Thank you so much for all of your thoughts and please pass on my heartfelt thank you to all who prayed.

Suggestion 7: Use healing prayer in evangelism

I believe with conviction that prayer for divine healing is one of the most powerful yet under-used resources we have in reaching the unchurched with the love of God. When those who are not yet Christians come into contact with the healing power of God, it has an amazing effect on their receptivity to the Gospel. In fact, we should always remember that the gifts of healing and miracles were meant to attend and confirm the Gospel message in the New Testament, and the same should be true today. The gifts serve the Gospel.

Here are some examples from very recent times of how divine healing in the name of Jesus has caused greater receptivity to the Gospel in the hearts of unchurched people, and opened up opportunities to share about Jesus. The first is an e-mail from a housewife and mother of five:

Dear Mark,

I have just skipped all the way to school and back (well, figuratively) because of the news given to me at the school gate! My non-Christian friend who came to the Friday night healing meeting underwent an operation yesterday to remove her ovaries and the cysts that had shown up on the scan prior to the meeting. When the consultant examined the lining of her womb, it was completely normal: no cysts, no polyps, nothing! Her husband said to me, 'My wife knows it was that evening that's done this!' 'I just knew you were going to tell me that,' I whooped. I can't contain this indescribable joy. This is the Good News of Jesus Christ: he heals TODAY!

The second very recent e-mail message is from the wife of a young man who dared to pray for a Muslim woman at work:

Dear Mark,

Just a quick testimony about a lady who is a colleague of my husband, Mike, at work. This lady in question is pregnant and Mike got chatting to her and asked how the pregnancy was going. She said that the baby was breech and that she was worried about it (this was at 35 weeks). She had a scan in a week's time. Mike shared with her my testimony about our baby Grace being breech and how we prayed and saw God turn the baby around at the last minute. So Mike asked her if she minded him praying for her that the baby would turn. So there and then in the foyer of the company HQ Mike prayed for her.

She came back a week later after her scan and said that the baby in her previous scan had been lying flat and in that position it wouldn't have been able to turn, but that it was now in the foetal position but still breech.

So we thanked the Lord for the change and prayed that the baby would turn all the way around. She met up with Mike today and told him that at her last scan the baby was now head down. God is in the business of turning things around. I thought you might be encouraged by that!

Pressing in for more of the miraculous

These suggestions are just suggestions. They are not meant to be an exhaustive list, nor are they meant to be the final word on the subject. The important thing is to get a healing ministry going in the local church and to do so through a properly trained and accountable team of appropriate people. Once you have done that, you will, if you are faithful and persistent, begin to see – over the course of time – many people healed through prayer offered in Jesus' name.

Having said that, I want to finish this chapter with one more thought: never be content with what you are seeing right now. Always press in with desperation and faith for God to do more by way of healings and miracles. As you look back, give thanks to the Father for all he has done over the months and years. Gratitude is vital in the healing ministry. But look forward as well. Ask the Father to do more than you have already seen. Ask him to heal cancers, remove tumours, restore limbs, heal the lame, and make blind eyes see and deaf ears hear. Pray this especially in the lives of those who are not yet Christians, that they may see that God is alive and that his Good News is really Good News!

Every so often we move into what I call Acts 4 prayer. This is the prayer prayed by the apostles and the early church in Jerusalem. It is recorded in Acts 4 and it occurs just after a great miracle, the healing of the lame man at the Beautiful Gate in the Temple precincts in Jerusalem. Many churches would have said, 'That's a great miracle, thank you Lord.' But the apostolic church responded to this event, and the opposition that was aroused by it, by praying 'More, Lord!' In other words, 'That was great, Lord. But can you do more?'

So we read that with one heart and mind they addressed the sovereign Lord of the universe and asked the following:

And now, O Lord, hear their threats, and give your servants great boldness in their preaching. Send your healing power; may miraculous signs and wonders be done through the name of your holy servant Jesus (Acts 4:29–30).

Luke records that at the end of this prayer the building shook and the believers (over five thousand in number) were all filled with the Holy Spirit and with boldness. In Acts 5 we also learn that God has indeed answered the prayer for more miraculous signs and wonders. Luke tells us in Acts 5:12 that 'the apostles were performing many miraculous signs and wonders among the people'.

I love the faith and fervency of these early Christians. They did not allow questions of 'theodicy' (why God allows suffering) to get in the way of their childlike faith. They did not allow liberal theology to cloud their judgment with scepticism. They simply believed that God would do miracles among them, prayed for the sovereign Lord to stretch out his hand, and then in due course witnessed signs and wonders.

My conviction is that there is so much more of God's miraculous power than we have seen. Have you ever noticed Acts 19:11, where Luke says the Lord did 'extraordinary miracles' (NIV) through Paul? What are 'extraordinary miracles'? We have rarely seen 'ordinary miracles' (if that isn't an oxymoron!). But we haven't even considered 'extraordinary miracles'. As we get nearer to the return of Jesus, as the Kingdom of God advances in greater strength, we should expect and pray for such 'extraordinary' miracles.

So begin to 'mind the gap' between the church 'then' and the church 'now', and dare to believe and pray for 'More, Lord!'

Chapter 7

Jesus, Our Example

MARC A. DUPONT

Jesus – the anointed one

Our supreme example of a biblical healer is always Jesus Christ. The name Christ means 'the anointed one', which in ancient times meant someone who had oil or ointment rubbed onto them as a sign of consecration. Luke chapter 3 describes how the Holy Spirit descended upon Jesus in bodily form after he had been baptized by John. In the following chapter Jesus quotes a prophecy concerning himself – given by Isaiah some seven hundred years previously. He states to the people of his home town:

> *The Spirit of the Lord is on me, because he has anointed me to preach good news to the poor. He has sent me to proclaim freedom for the prisoners and recovery of sight for the blind, to release the oppressed (Lk. 4:18, NIV).*

The Holy Spirit was deeply 'rubbed' into Jesus in the same way that a measure of perfume or moisturizing cream might be rubbed into you or me – rubbed into us so much that it *flows* from us. The evidence of this anointing was the absolutely amazing amount of continual healings and miracles he performed.

Jesus placed a very great value on these works of power. When asked by Philip to show him the Father, Jesus responded by saying:

The words that I say to you I do not speak on my own initiative, but the Father abiding in me does his works. Believe me that I am in the Father and the Father is in me; otherwise believe because of the works themselves (Jn. 14:10–11).

Jesus was very willing to let the acts he did by the power of the Holy Spirit testify to his deity and his message. In fact, when some of the people wanted to stone Jesus, in John 10:32, Jesus replied, 'I showed you many good works from the Father; for which of them are you stoning me?' He was more than happy to let his actions speak for him.

When John the Baptist was imprisoned and soon to be martyred, he sent some of his disciples to question Jesus as to whether he was, in fact, the Messiah (Lk. 7:19–20). What Jesus didn't say in response to the question is just as important as what he did say. He responded:

Go and report to John what you have seen and heard: the blind receive sight, the lame walk, the lepers are cleansed, and the deaf hear, the dead are raised up, the poor have the gospel preached to them (Lk. 7:22).

What he did not say was, 'Take to John a copy of my seventeen-point doctoral dissertation.' Neither did he say, 'Take to John my latest tape series.' He did not even reply, 'Yes, I am the Messiah.' He simply let his actions speak for themselves: acts not only of supernatural power, but also of great compassion.

One of the reasons the Gospel is advancing so prolifically in continents such as Asia, South America and Africa is that for the most part, the body of Christ in those parts of the world wholeheartedly believes that God wants to do the same sorts of healings and miracles today as he did some two thousand years ago. In the western world, by contrast, we have reduced the Gospel message to words alone, almost devoid of the power of the Holy Spirit. While it is true that a healing or miracle in North America will not have the same sort of ripple effect for the Gospel as in a poor region of Mozambique, it cannot be denied that we have received the same Holy Spirit who does these great works of power.

A friend of mine who pastors in Ohio accompanied me on a ministry trip to Mozambique and Malawi. He was greatly gripped by the healings and miracles experienced by sick, diseased and lame people while on that trip. He took an afternoon off and stayed behind at the compound where we were sleeping in order to pray. He prayed from his heart to God about his conviction that his city in Ohio needed the Kingdom of God to move in power as it did in Africa. While praying, he recognized that there was more faith for the supernatural in Africa, as well as greater widespread poverty, which, in a sense, forced more people to seek God more wholeheartedly. The Lord responded that while all that was true, he had given the same Holy Spirit to his children in Ohio as he had to his children in Africa. Since that time, there have been many, many healings in my friend's church. Several of these healings have been very dramatic, such as eyes being healed.

The Apostle Paul stated to the church in Corinth that although God gave different supernatural gifts to different people, it was the same Holy Spirit who performed all of these things (1 Cor. 12:11). I believe, in fact, that the Holy Spirit is the most under-utilized resource in the contemporary church. Let's look at how Jesus worked with and related to the Holy Spirit.

The Person, the Presence and His Power

First of all, we must recognize that the Holy Spirit is the third person of the Trinity. It is well beyond the scope of this book to do a proper study of the Trinity of God. However, let's look at what the Apostle Paul stated concerning the Holy Spirit to the church of Corinth. In his second letter to the Corinthians, he wrote:

The Lord is the Spirit, and where the Spirit of the Lord is, there is liberty (2 Cor. 3:17).

While Jesus is at the Father's right hand receiving adoration from the angels and love from the Father, he is also very much with his people. In the very last verse of the Gospel of Matthew he told the disciples:

I am with you always, even to the end of the age (Mt. 28:20).

But then a short time later many witnesses saw him ascending on a cloud to the Father. Was he lying? No, absolutely not. It was necessary, however, for him to die on the Cross and pay for our sins, and then return to the Father in order that he could send forth his presence – his Holy Spirit – to accomplish two essential things. First, that his Spirit could inhabit each person who submits his or her life to the Lordship of Christ. And secondly, so that there could be an army of little 'Christs', or 'anointed ones'. So instead of Jesus, as one individual, walking the face of the earth restoring broken hearts and lives, there could be a future army of millions empowered and led by the Holy Spirit to do the things Jesus did.

When the twelve disciples came back from their first ministry trip, they were excited about the miracles and deliverances they had seen the Holy Spirit do through them. Jesus said in response:

I was watching Satan fall from heaven like lightning (Lk. 10:18).

The reason why Satan, or, as he's known, the 'prince of the power of the air' (Eph. 2:2), was falling is that all of a sudden he realized his kingdom of death, lies and suffering was about to be overcome. Jesus came preaching that the Kingdom of God was at hand. And as the disciples began to demonstrate how this future army of 'little Christs' would go about destroying the works of his evil empire, Satan began to see the beginning of his own demise.

Until the Cross, many individuals could have an 'anointing' or capacity from God to accomplish a certain job or function for the Lord. We see this with the prophets, some of the kings, the craftsmen who worked in the tabernacle of Moses, etc. But as Jesus stated to the disciples in John 16:7, it was to their benefit that he allow himself to be crucified and then go to the Father in order that he might send forth the counsellor, or helper (the Holy Spirit), to all who would call on his name.

The Holy Spirit is much more than simply an ethereal feeling or a spiritual power or force. Neither is he simply a spirit, in the sense of the angelic realm. The Holy Spirit is the Spirit of adoption, or 'sonship', whom we receive in our hearts when we give our lives to God. He is the very presence of God in the world today. In a broad generalization, we could say that he wants primarily to do three things in our lives. First, as the Apostle Paul referred to him in Romans 8:15, he is the Spirit of adoption. He continually wants to bring us into an ever-deepening relationship with God the Father and the person of Jesus. As Jesus stated, he (the Holy Spirit) will not speak on his own initiative, but rather he will disclose the things of the Father and Jesus to us (Jn. 16:13). Secondly, he wants to lead and guide us into the fullness of God's will for our lives. As Paul stated in Romans 8:14, 'All who are being led by the Spirit of God, these are sons of God' (and that also includes women). Thirdly, the Holy Spirit wants to empower or anoint us for ministry in such a way that we might minister to people as Jesus did. For the sake of our study concerning healing, we will examine the leading and anointing of the Holy Spirit in Jesus' life.

We know that when the Virgin Mary asked the angel Gabriel how it was possible that she, a virgin, could give birth to a child, Gabriel responded:

> *The Holy Spirit will come upon you, and the power of the Most High will overshadow you; and for that reason the holy child shall be called the Son of God (Lk. 1:35).*

So it is safe to say that Jesus' very beginning as fully God *and* fully man was when the Holy Spirit moved on a person's life. Next, we will jump to some thirty-one years later. Jesus, who knew no sin, allowed himself to be baptized by John, who was preaching repentance of sins and the coming of the Kingdom of God. When Jesus came up out of the water, three significant things took place. First, the Father spoke his approval over the Son. He was well pleased with the humility and character of Jesus. Secondly, the heavens opened. This indicated that with the life of Jesus there would be no barrier to the fullness of what God in heaven desired to do on earth. So it can be with each of his sons and daughters. The more we submit our hearts and lives to the ways of God, the more we can walk in great freedom, so that the blessings of heaven might be on earth. And thirdly, the Holy Spirit came on Jesus as a dove. This, we can say, refers to the anointing or empowering of the Holy Spirit.

The anointing

As we seek to imitate the life of Jesus by doing the types of things he did, it is critical that we understand and experience the anointing of the Holy Spirit. The anointing of the Holy Spirit is something distinct from the initial filling of the Holy Spirit. When we give our lives to Christ Jesus we receive the Holy Spirit *within*. When we receive the gifting and anointing of the Holy Spirit, we have the Holy Spirit *upon* us. For example, if we look at the apostles prior to the Cross, we know that they experienced the anointing or power of God in their lives. This is evidenced by the fact that they went out two by two and performed miracles and healings and cast out demons as they preached the Gospel. They were operating in the anointing of God's power on their lives. It was the same for the prophets before them, for many of God's messengers, and for various people whom God raised up to serve him. For example, we read about Bezalel:

> *I have filled him with the Spirit of God in wisdom, in understanding, in knowledge, and in all kinds of craftsmanship, to make artistic designs for work in gold, in silver, and in bronze, and in the cutting of stones for settings, and in the carving of wood, that he may work in all kinds of craftsmanship (Ex. 31:3–5).*

Or Joshua, who led the Hebrew people across the Jordan River into the Promised Land:

> *Now Joshua the son of Nun was filled with the spirit of wisdom, for Moses had laid his hands on him; and the sons of Israel listened to him and did as the LORD had commanded Moses (Deut. 34:9).*

The word for 'spirit' in this passage is the Hebrew *ruach*, which is used throughout the Old Testament for the Holy Spirit and can be translated as the 'breath of God'. The Old Testament scriptures are filled with illustrations of God anointing people with the power and gifts of the Holy Spirit in order to carry out his will.

The power of the Cross, however, meant that men and women could have an entirely different relationship with God, because our sins had been paid for. From the fall in the Garden of Eden up to the Cross, deep, abiding, continual intimacy with God was not possible because of our sins. But when we embrace the Cross, our sins are separated from us as far as the east is from the west. Intimacy with God through the 'Spirit of adoption' is now possible. This is why Jesus invited us in John 15 to 'abide in him'.

John 20:22 records how, in his first meeting with the disciples after the resurrection, Jesus 'breathed on them'. He released the *ruach* or 'breath of God' into them. Up to that point they had known the person of Jesus and the anointing of the Holy Spirit. But now, something truly remarkable is taking place. Their sins have now been paid for, and so they can become 'born again', with the 'Spirit of adoption' coming within them. For the sake of our focus on healing we will call this the first and primary filling of the Holy Spirit in a believer's life. This is the all-important Holy Spirit within.

There is a secondary filling, which does not have quite so much to do with intimacy, although it does very much help foster that. This is the 'anointing' or 'empowering' of the Holy Spirit upon our lives to enable us to serve God as true sons and daughters. This is what Jesus was referring to when he instructed the disciples in Acts 1:8:

> *You will receive power when the Holy Spirit has come upon you; and you shall be my witnesses both in Jerusalem, and in all Judea and Samaria, and even to the remotest part of the earth.*

When it comes to emulating the life of Jesus, good intentions, discipline and stalwart resolution are helpful, but not enough. As the prophet Zechariah stated:

'Not by might nor by power, but by my Spirit,' says the LORD *of hosts (Zech. 4:6).*

For any service or ministry to people truly to have an eternal impact, it must be done in the power and anointing of the Holy Spirit. That does not mean that our effort is not required: it is, but beyond that there must be the anointing of God in our lives. We see this exemplified in the fierce battles in which God gave victory to the Hebrew army against their enemies. They still had to go out to the battlefield and swing their swords, throw their spears and hold up their shields. But, as with Gideon and his three hundred men defeating a great army of tens of thousands, the battle belonged to the Lord. When it comes to contemporary ministry, mere eloquence and clever strategies are not enough. No one comes to God unless first drawn by the Spirit.

When Jesus left the Jordan River after being baptized by John, both Matthew 4:1 and Luke 4:1 tell us Jesus was 'led by the Holy Spirit' into the wilderness. After his forty days of fasting and testing by the devil, Luke 4:14 says, 'Jesus returned to Galilee in the power of the Spirit.' From the time of his baptism to his ascension to the Father, Jesus was *led by the Holy Spirit* and *ministered in the power of the Holy Spirit*.

It is of critical importance for us to grasp the relevance of Jesus being led and empowered by the Holy Spirit, for the simple reason that he calls us to do the same. That is to say, he calls us to do what is impossible in our own ability, but possible in his Spirit. Jesus, the fully God and fully man being, played by the same sort of rules that you and I have to play by. He could easily have healed people in his own power. After all, he created everything that exists (Col. 1:16). Also, he could easily have operated by his omniscience – his all-knowing of the past, the present and the future – but he didn't. He could have done both those things, but he chose to limit himself to our limitations. Hebrews 4:15 says:

> *For we do not have a high priest who cannot sympathize with our weaknesses ...*

Although the primary application of this verse has to do with Jesus never sinning, a secondary application is that while being fully God, he lived as a normal man while on earth – very much in tune with our weaknesses, both our weaknesses deriving from our fallen state and our weaknesses as humans in general. He did so in order to be a High Priest we can relate to. Just as he invited the disciples of two thousand years ago to 'come along and do what I do', so he invites us today. And the wonderful thing is he never asks us to do what we can't do. Rather, he invites us to do the impossible by the power and leading of his Holy Spirit. So, we read these words of the apostle Paul:

> *I can do all things through him who strengthens me (Phil. 4:13).*

By the power and leading of God's own Holy Spirit we can, from time to time, leave our realm of 'impossibilities' and experience God's Kingdom on earth as it is in heaven.

One of the creative miracles I saw the Lord do in the 1980s is a helpful illustration. A woman brought her young son, who had a clubfoot, to me for prayer at the end of a meeting. In fact, it was the last of four nightly meetings held while I was visiting a church in the mid-west of the United States. After four nights of extensive ministry I was very tired. So when she showed me his foot with the obvious deformity, my tiredness took over and I felt no faith whatsoever to pray for this five- or six-year-old boy. As she explained that he could walk OK, but had never been able to run successfully in his life, my heart went out to him, but I still felt my tiredness upon me. To step into a faith mode and believe for the impossible seemed even more impossible at that point in time. However, as I knelt down and began to pray for his foot, almost immediately right in front of my eyes it began to change shape. What had, more or less, appeared as a block of wood covered by skin began to change into a normal foot with toes, an arch etc, all in normal size and shape. It had taken place so quickly that I was a bit dizzy. I wasn't sure whether I was actually seeing a miracle happen, or was imagining it. It took all of about five seconds for the transition to take place. The young boy immediately began running around the room. He was running perfectly for the first time in his life. His mother was jumping up and down and yelling out. I was still kneeling down on the floor, trying to lay hands on this foot that was no longer there. I was in a bit of shock. I hadn't 'felt' anything supernatural, or any power whatsoever. That is precisely what Zechariah meant, however, when he stated, 'not by might (of man), nor by power (of our own), but by the Holy Spirit'.

As humans with our ups and downs, good days and bad days, we do not always feel good, or spiritual, or seem to be in a place where we can really be a blessing to people. But as we walk through the doors of opportunity that God gives us for his Kingdom, we step beyond ourselves, and our possibilities, and into the Kingdom of God and the impossible. This is the empowering with which Jesus promised the apostles and the church they will serve him.

The Holy Spirit and creativity

One of the basic reasons why we desperately need the leading of the Holy Spirit is for the sake of creativity. By creativity I do not mean merely in the arts, although the Holy Spirit does work through the creative gifts he gives to some. What I mean is doing things in God's freedom and 'style'. When we look at the some of the craftsmanship of God on earth, we see such amazing diversity. There are no two snowflakes alike, no two mountains alike, and no leaves exactly alike. In travelling to many countries around the world I have had the privilege of visiting many, many beaches. I was raised for the most part in San Diego, California, which has some of the most beautiful beaches in the world. I have seen wonderful beaches in Africa, Scandinavia and Hawaii. They are all, however, distinct in their beauty. For example, the beaches on some small islands off the coast of Mozambique seem almost like paradise (at least our understanding of paradise), whereas some beaches I visited one summer in the far north of Norway, while equally stunning, were dramatically different. Those beaches in Mozambique looked just like some of the classic poster images of beaches in places like Tahiti. The beach in Norway, however, was majestic with its dark sands offset by mountain peaks, huge rocks and big skies. It seemed more like a 'moonscape' than the kind of beach I was used to. Was one better than another? No, beauty is in the eyes of the beholder. It is all the creativity of God. God, I like to say, is the 'creator of creativity'. And in everything he does he involves creativity.

In contrast to God, however, we humans tend to be creatures of comfort that love to fall into the trap of traditions. Once we experience success in a particular area, we try to replicate or duplicate that experience in order to achieve the same sort of breakthrough or success. God is just the opposite. While he is the same yesterday, today and forever in his values and attributes, he delights in doing the things he does in such unique ways. For example, each human being has highly distinct eyes, fingerprints and vocal cords. God is not a utilitarian artist who does things on a mass production basis. On the contrary, he is the ultimate artist.

When we look at Jesus healing people of blindness, we see him ministering in a variety of ways. In the account of the two blind men healed, found in Matthew 9, Jesus merely touched their eyes and spoke to them. Mark 8:22–26 tells us that Jesus spat in a blind man's eyes and then laid hands on his eyes and the man was healed. In the account found in John 9:1–9, we see Jesus doing something different again. This time he spat in the dirt and made some clay, or mud. He then put the mud in the man's eyes and directed him to go and wash in the pool called Siloam. When the man did so and came back to Jesus, he could see.

How the Holy Spirit uses us one day might be completely different to the next. This is for two basic reasons. First it is to help us stay in a posture of dependency on him, rather than trusting in a method we've established. Secondly, God loves to move in creative ways – it's part of his very nature. For example, when I first learned to pray for the sick in the early 1980s I very much stuck to the 'Five Step Model'. After a while, however, I began to find that I had reduced that model to a method, rather than using it as a foundation or launching pad. In the mid-1980s I was ministering with a team in Mexico City for several nights. By the grace of God, we were seeing many extraordinary healings each night. On the third night I sensed the Lord wanted to heal people with eye diseases or blindness. When I gave the word, some fifteen people with varying degrees of blindness or diseased eyes came forward. I had been having people come forward for prayer and then having the ministry team with me pray for them. Afterwards we would have people who had been healed testify. On this occasion, however, the Lord led me to bring them up onto the stage and told me to pray for them simply by touching each of them lightly on the head, without praying for them individually. This style of 'one man show' ministry very much went against the grain of what I was used to. I, and most of my good friends in ministry, would have equated that with the old style of the 'man of God' ministry, whereas we were very much into the team concept. To my surprise, however, after I had quickly walked by each of them, simply touching each of them on the top of the forehead, thirteen of the fifteen were completely healed. It wasn't a matter of God not being into the team ministry, or the Five Step Model, but rather that he is completely free in how he likes to work. My problem had been that I had made a monument at the other end of the scale from the 'one man ministry' model.

Words of knowledge

It is very critical that we learn to develop 'ears to hear what the Spirit is saying', not only for the sake of knowing God's direction in our lives, but also so that we might minister to people in the way the Holy Spirit desires us to. Part of the leading of the Holy Spirit when it comes to healing and evangelism is the gift of the word of knowledge (1 Cor. 12:8). The gift of the word of knowledge is vitally important if we are to pray for the root problem rather than the surface symptom. Otherwise, we can end up merely putting a band-aid on a person who's really in need of surgery, metaphorically speaking.

Many afflictions people live with today are due to things like high stress levels, long-term unforgiveness, generational curses and, of course, the demonic. As the healing movement began to become more widespread in the early days of the Charismatic movement, there was sometimes in evidence a rather simplistic theology towards people who were not healed after receiving prayer. For example, someone who did not receive a healing might be told that they were 'in sin', or they simply 'did not have enough faith'. As for the first reason, sometimes that is true, but many times it is not. On one occasion the disciples asked Jesus whether a man's blindness was due to his own personal sin or that of his parents. Jesus responded:

> *It was neither that this man sinned, nor his parents; but it was so that the works of God might be displayed in him (Jn. 9:3).*

Sometimes we just don't know, and it can be dangerous to assume we have the full mind of Christ on any particular person's situation. And as to the charge that some who receive prayer but are not healed don't have faith, to that I say 'hogwash'. The fact that they have come forward for prayer in a meeting or have asked for prayer means they have faith. On several occasions, people wanting prayer, who were suffering tremendous problems, have said to me after explaining their problems, 'I don't have much faith.' My response is, 'Of course you have faith. If you did not have faith, you would not have been open to prayer.' We must remember that Jesus never said we need faith the size of a mountain to move a mustard seed. Rather, he said if we had just a little faith (a mustard seed), a mountain could be removed. And in the Hebrew culture of that day, a mountain was a metaphor for a serious problem or trial.

There are afflictions, however, which are sometimes rooted in personal sin, such as unforgiveness. There are sometimes also inherited sicknesses, rather like a generational curse that needs to be broken in the name of Jesus. However, I think some healing ministries focus too much on generational curses. The only place in the Bible where we see any significant mention of generational curses is in the books of Moses – the Mosaic covenant. In the New

Covenant, through Christ Jesus, we have a new heritage from God the Father. Sometimes, however, we need to 'appropriate' the blood of the Lamb over areas of our life that our enemy, the demonic realm, may feel it has a right to, as a result of afflicting our families for generations with the same curse. Just as we have physical and personality traits that we inherit from our parents, so too we inherit spiritual blessings and curses. And just as the Apostle James tells us that we often do not have because we do not ask, so sometimes we have unfavourable things in our lives because we do not take authority in the name of Jesus. The devil and his horde of minions will gladly wreak havoc in an area of a believer's life if they get the chance. And since the devil is a liar (Jn. 8:44), he will gladly abide as an illegal tenant unless the landlord (you and I) along with the police (Jesus) evict him.

A particular bondage of sin, however, can open the door into the demonic realm, resulting in health problems. Those problems can be in the emotional and/or the physical realm. Jesus gave a powerful illustration of the negative effects of choosing to harbour unforgiveness or bitterness towards others in Matthew 18. In the parable of the Unmerciful Servant, found in verses 23–35, Jesus told of a servant who owed his king a great deal of money. The king chose to forgive the servant his entire debt when he asked for mercy. But then that same servant went after others who owed him sums that were trifling in comparison to what he had owed the master. And when they could not pay him, he had them thrown into a debtors' prison. When the king found out about the lack of mercy on the part of the servant towards others, he was 'moved with anger' and 'handed him over to the torturers' (Mt. 18:34). So it is in the life of anyone, especially a Christian, who practises the sin of unforgiveness towards another in his or her heart.

The consequences of practising any sin can also be devastating for our overall health. We need to place an emphasis on the word 'practising', because the Bible makes it clear that none of us is perfect. However, when we make room for a particular sin in our life by practising it – doing it over and over again – we open the door, to a degree, to the demonic realm. Particular demons have particular assignments and manifestations. And when a person gives room to the demonic realm through ongoing unconfessed sin, a very real physical and/or emotional problem can result. The Apostle Paul stated:

> *Let us also lay aside every encumbrance and the sin which so easily entangles us (Heb. 12:1).*

In the life of a Christian, we are not speaking of becoming 'demonically possessed'. That only occurs in the life of an individual who has surrendered almost all control in their lives to evil. The man in the Gospel who had a 'legion' (a huge number) of demons was the great exception, not the norm.

What can occur in the life of a Christian, however, is that there can be a room, or rooms, in the mansion of their life that is not swept out and in good order. We have many 'rooms' or areas of involvement in our lives – our relationships, our thought life, our dreams, our careers, etc. When you buy a large, previously owned house, the whole house and property belong to you, but there might be rooms or cupboards where there are cobwebs, dirt and refuse left over from the previous tenant. When we surrender our lives to Christ Jesus, he becomes the legal owner of our lives. But in the lifelong process of sanctification and consecration we learn to yield more effectively every area of our lives to him. In a sense, some rooms are cleaned out and given fresh paint and wallpaper before others. And if we leave a certain room under the influence of the old tenant, the consequences can be bad for the whole house. So although a Christian who belongs to God cannot be 'demon-possessed', they can have areas or rooms in their lives that are under an alien and evil influence.

So there are those physical and emotional problems that are a direct result of sin in a person's life. There are sometimes also generational curses that need to be broken. But much of the time sicknesses and accidents happen merely because we are all part of a fallen people. As Jesus said, the rain falls on the good and the bad. Since a sickness can stem from so many differing sources, the gift of the word of knowledge, as well as the gift of the word of wisdom, is very much needed for an effective healing ministry. That is not to say God does not heal without specific words as to the cause of a problem, because he certainly does heal in a great variety of ways through a great variety of people. However, when it comes to being as effective as possible in serving people, like a master carpenter we want the full toolbox at hand and we want to be well trained with those tools. Hence, we continually need the leading and input, as well as the power, of the precious Holy Spirit. We also need the Holy Spirit's creativity and timing in ministry. To live an effective lifestyle of seeking first the Kingdom of God we must learn to live a life that is yielded to and filled with the Holy Spirit. The great thing is, however, that God very much desires to fill us with his Spirit and encourage and enable us to come into ever-increasing abundant life. Jesus tells us that if we, being evil (not fully whole) know how to give good gifts to our children, how much more will the Father give us the Holy Spirit (Lk. 11:13). As Peter did when he saw Jesus walking on the water, we too are free to say, 'Can I come along too?' His response is always a resounding 'Yes'!

Chapter 8

The Call to Persevere

MARC A. DUPONT

To persevere: to persist, to keep at something, to keep trying, to not give up.

Grace: a gift, something that you do not deserve.

God is sovereign! That means that God is in complete control of what he desires to do, any time he desires to do it. Within the context of his sovereignty, however, he also allows people free will. In a nutshell, this explains why a loving God would allow violence and tragedy to take place. He honours the fact that humans, created in his image, have the capacity to make decisions, just as he does. We can, in fact, make decisions for good or for evil. In his sovereignty, or absolute control, he also allows each of us to exercise our free will in such a way that we can either qualify, or disqualify, ourselves with regard to his blessings and intended destiny for our lives.

Healing is always a grace, or gift, from God. If we can understand that 'Jehovah Rapha', or the 'Lord God who heals us', is a God who loves to heal simply because he is good and filled with compassion and grace, we can comprehend that healing is always a gift of God, each and every time it happens. As James stated:

Every good thing given and every perfect gift is from above, coming down from the Father of lights (Jas. 1:17).

Equally true, however, is the fact that healing is not a programme.

God allows himself and his blessings to be accessed by faith. Faith, however, is much more than simply a positive mindset. Faith is determining that our actions, attitudes, relationships and goals will be governed by our belief in the goodness of God. Hebrews 11:6 says:

Without faith it is impossible to please him, for he who comes to God must believe that he is and that he is a rewarder of those who seek him.

As has been said before, 'Faith is believing God, and working hard.' Healing is a grace or gift from God, but we often have to play our part in being the recipient of that gift. On the other hand, because God is all about relationship, his arm cannot be twisted into action merely because we pray the right-sounding prayer or claim a particular verse of the Bible. All this is to say that while faith is necessary, applied faith does not negate the mystery or sovereignty of God. We dare not fall into the trap of using the truths, precepts and concepts of the Bible to make demands on God with little or no regard for him being God Almighty. As in many other areas, such as being a God of both mercy and holiness, he is the God of the both/and. We cannot earn the gifts of God, simply because they are gifts. On the other hand he calls for our hearts to be in a constant posture of faith, to the degree that we would seek after him for what he desires to give us. Not to do so can cause us to miss out on what he has for us. As the Apostle James also wrote:

You do not have because you do not ask (Jas. 4:2).

God is a God of mystery, and so Jesus, as we saw in Chapter 7, was led by the Spirit. Churches and Bible teachers that focus solely on the truths of the Bible are very hesitant to move into the realm of the power and prophetic gifts of the Holy Spirit, because those gifts necessitate that one learn to operate out of intimacy with God, or heart knowledge, rather than strictly governing one's life by methodology. I remember a situation that occurred one night while I was ministering to a number of people at the end of a meeting. I was giving some words of prophetic encouragement that the Lord was giving me for a few of them, when a pastor from another church came up to me with a great deal of indignation. He demanded to know why I supposed I should be telling people about what God intended for their future. His consternation stemmed from the fact that in his church circles they did not study the spiritual gifts for the church as outlined by the Apostle Paul in 1 Corinthians 12 and 14. They were completely unaware of the fact that God often desires to speak inspired words to the church today, to encourage us in his will for our lives. He had a great deal of trouble accepting the biblical concept of God speaking today! His perception of the Bible was that it was a set of guidelines for a successful life here on earth and in preparation for eternal life in heaven to come. While the Bible is a manual for successful life, it is also much more than that. It is an invitation into a great relationship with the living God and an invitation to the grand adventure of a Holy Spirit-led life. We must remember that God is God the Father, God the Son and God the Holy Spirit. He is not God the Father, God the Son and God the Holy Bible. Jesus is the *truth himself* – he is much more than simply a written set of truths *about* God.

When God's ears seem deaf

Since God is a person and not merely a set of precepts and concepts, we must trust in him and his goodness regardless of how or when he chooses to answer our prayer requests. There are some basic and essential needs that God will usually consistently meet on an everyday basis, such as the need for daily food. David wrote in Psalm 37:25:

> *I have been young and now I am old, yet I have not seen the righteous forsaken or his descendants begging bread.*

On the other hand, there can be a great need in our lives to which it seems God turns a deaf ear. Does that mean God does not desire to meet that need? No, it absolutely does not. Rather it means either that God in his wisdom desires to meet it in some other way that we can't imagine, or simply that the timing is not now.

Many of us in the western world suffer from the inability to distinguish between our needs and our desires. While God does desire to fulfil those desires of our heart that are good and righteous, often our dreams and visions need to be pruned of things like selfishness, ambition and envy. The desire for good health, however, is one area of life that God is deeply committed to. In general, we can say that healing is part of the package of the atonement in Christ Jesus. As Isaiah prophesied about the redemption in Christ Jesus, 'by his scourging we are healed' (Is. 53:5). Our dilemma, though, is not whether God desires to heal us, but rather when and how he desires to do so.

A second problem that we people of a western mind-set suffer from is that we are highly uncomfortable with intellectual dichotomies, or tensions that seem to be conflicting. For example, I heard years ago about a famous international missions school located in the United States.

The student body consisted of missionaries and future missionaries from all over the globe. In an attempt to try to understand why the churches in Africa and Asia seemed to experience so much more of the power of God in healings and miracles, all the students were asked to answer a series of questions. One of the questions went like this: 'Cotton only grows in warm climates. England has a cold climate. Therefore, can cotton grow in England?' Overwhelmingly the students from North America and Europe responded, 'No, if England has a cold climate and cotton can only grow in a warm climate, cotton cannot grow in England.' In complete contrast, the students from Africa and Asia overwhelmingly responded. 'I don't know; I have never been to England.' The western students were willing to take a stand based on what they could intellectually understand by stated precepts. The African and Asian students were not willing to discount something simply because the stated facts were in contrast. They wanted experiential knowledge. When Jesus said that to experience the Kingdom we must become both converted and childlike, he was directly addressing this problem facing western Christians in the modern age. Unlike the early church of Acts, we have lost our sense of 'awe and wonder' about the person of the Holy Spirit. Obviously the natural laws of health, nutrition and science are all applicable to a health problem and should be considered. After all, the principles by which doctors treat the human body are based on what God established. But we are also born into the Kingdom of God, where God's power for the miraculous can be accessed and experienced. It was God, after all, who established the natural laws, such as gravity, that govern the universe. But beyond that, it was the supernatural that created the natural, not the other way round. In giving our lives to Christ Jesus, we are now part of the both/and. We are part of this natural realm for as long as we occupy these human bodies. But we are also now part of the Kingdom of God, which is beyond the limitations of the natural. This is to say there will be, or at least should be, times and occasions when a Christian experiences the supernatural power of God overriding the natural laws of this world, for example when a lung which the doctors know is destroyed by cancer is completely healed after prayer. In documented cases of 'unexplainable miracles', Doctor Jesus has tended the patient. As his representatives we should, at least occasionally, see his mighty heart and hand at work breaking past the known possibilities of human abilities.

Persevering prayer

In essence there are four basic ways in which healing is accessed and/or released. The first two have to do with the individual in need of healing taking the initiative, when a sick individual cries out to God. There are countless testimonies of God hearing those prayers and simply healing the person. Alternatively, a person can either go to someone who has the God-given gift of healing or, as James wrote, go to the elders of a church and ask for prayer for healing (and one can also ask prayer ministry teams in a congregation for prayer). In the economy of God's grace and mercy he allows us at times to make a demand upon the anointing of a gifted person, or on the spiritual authority he gives to church leaders.

The third and fourth ways are God-initiated. For example, when in a church meeting or a seemingly chance encounter with an individual, someone who has the gift of healing is given a word of knowledge and directed by God to minister healing to a person. This is what happened when God spoke to Ananias in Acts 9:10–12, telling him to go to Saul of Tarsus and pray for him so that he might regain his sight. A while ago, while I was speaking at a church in Bergen, Norway, the Lord gave me a word in the midst of the meeting that there was a woman present in severe stomach pain, who had already had operations and was still very ill. I actually stopped what I was focused on at that point in the meeting and gave the word. A young woman came forward with that very problem and we prayed for her. Immediately the stomach pain, which had been so very bad that for weeks she could hardly walk, completely left her. She was completely healed.

The fourth type of healing is simply when a person is in a church meeting or a worship service, or perhaps an evangelistic outreach, where there is a tremendous presence of the Lord and wonderful things begin to happen sovereignly. A while back in my home church, during an extended worship service a woman visitor who was scheduled to have an operation on her hands felt the presence of God come over her. When she left the meeting, her hands were completely healed! Often, however, when God releases healing in the third or fourth way, he is doing so in response to ongoing prayer from the one in need of healing.

One of the problems of our generation today is that we seem to want everything immediately, without much of a price tag attached. Nothing truly worth having comes without some kind of fight. And the greater the prize, the more resistance we are likely to encounter – resistance without and, often, resistance within. Previous generations seemed to better understand the concept of sowing and then in the proper time reaping from our efforts. Jesus stated in Luke 11:9–10:

Ask, and it will be given to you; seek, and you will find; knock, and it will be opened to you. For everyone who asks, receives; and he who seeks, finds; and to him who knocks, it will be opened.

Faith in God is always critically important. Hebrews 11:6 says:

> *And without faith it is impossible to please him, for he who comes to God must believe that he is and that He is a rewarder of those who seek him.*

Choosing not to exercise faith can disqualify us from the blessings and promises of God.

The Bible is filled with stories of men and women who have led lives characterized by persevering faith which resulted in 'persevering prayer'. By persevering prayer we do not necessarily mean praying non-stop, but rather, not giving up on what God has put in their hearts. Not giving up, despite outward difficulties. One such story begins in Luke 8:43. Luke tells of a woman who had suffered with an ongoing haemorrhage for some twelve years. The passage tells us that she 'could not be healed by anyone'. Luke 8:40 says that Jesus had returned to the cities of Israel from the land of the Gerasenes. As he was praying for many of the people, this woman came up behind him and touched the fringe of his cloak, and immediately her haemorrhage stopped. Jesus said, 'Who is the one who touched me?' And while they were all denying it, Peter said, 'Master, the people are crowding and pressing in on you.' But Jesus said, 'Someone did touch me, for I was aware that power had gone out of me.' When the woman saw that she had not escaped notice, she came trembling and fell down before him, and declared in the presence of all the people the reason why she had touched him, and how she had been immediately healed. Then Jesus said to her, 'Daughter, your faith has made you well; go in peace.' This woman was practising 'persevering faith'.

The Gospel of Mark relates a similar story in chapter 2. It begins in verse 1:

*When he [Jesus] had come back to Capernaum several days after-
ward, it was heard that he was at home. And many were gathered
together, so that there was no longer room, not even near the door;
and he was speaking the word to them. And they came, bringing
to him a paralytic, carried by four men. Being unable to get to him
because of the crowd, they removed the roof above him; and when
they had dug an opening, they let down the pallet on which the
paralytic was lying. And Jesus seeing their faith said to the paralytic,
'Son, your sins are forgiven' (Mk. 2:1–5).*

When the religious leaders present strongly questioned
Jesus' authority to forgive sins, he went on to demonstrate
his authority by healing the man of his paralysis. The
paralytic ended up receiving both a physical and spiritual
healing due to the persevering faith of the four friends.

Living in an age characterized by a need for instant
gratification and instant success, when we labour hard and
do not immediately reap our desired goals, we tend to give
up. When praying for a healing or a breakthrough that only
God can bring about, we say to ourselves, 'Well, I guess it's
just not the will of God.' But the woman with the chronic
haemorrhage and the four friends of the paralysed man
refused to give up in their pursuit of healing. They were
not treating God as an errand boy; rather they were trusting
in his compassion and power to bless them. And they
persevered when they met with obstacles. We commonly
think of 'presumptuous prayer' as praying for extravagant
and unnecessary things. While those prayers may, indeed,
be presumptuous, we often presume on God in a negative
way by not truly praying for his best for our lives.

God's children and spiritual warfare

An aspect of persevering faith that must be discussed is
the fact that the devil hates the sons and daughters of

God. At one point, before his fall, Satan was the greatest of all the created beings. He was the most beautiful, the most wise, and perhaps the most gifted of the angelic race. Ezekiel 28:14 leads us to believe that he was the chief of the worshipping angels surrounding the throne of God. When he became more enamoured with himself than with the person of God, however, he was cast down from the mountain of the Lord and away from God's presence. Psalm 8:2 tells us that God has replaced the worship of the devil with that of humans who are as babes in comparison to the wisdom, strength and beauty that the devil once had, and to a degree still possesses. For that reason (and others) the devil hates humans – especially those who have given their lives to Christ and are worshippers of God. He views us as usurpers. While Jesus came to give us life super-abundantly, the devil came to rob, kill and destroy. And while not all sickness is directly related to a demon, some sickness and problems are purely spiritual warfare. In those cases especially, anyone who prays for the sick, or for healing of their own sickness, must know both their authority in Christ and the heart of Christ.

One of the most unusual words of knowledge I have experienced while praying for a sick person happened many years ago in Europe. Towards the end of a meeting, a lady came up for prayer. Since becoming a Christian a few years previously she had developed a problem with her foot. She could no longer walk long distances or stand for more than several minutes without experiencing significant pain in her foot. After speaking with her a few minutes I asked her the basic questions – had she experienced any accidents, what did the X-rays show, and so on – but she said she had not had any accidents, and the X-rays showed no problem.

So I began to pray. I specifically asked the Holy Spirit to show me if this was purely spiritual warfare. I then began to see in the spirit a small impish demon about the size of a small doll standing on her foot, mocking me. Demons are very territorial and are constantly looking for a person, or body part or soul, to own or possess. After speaking to the woman and praying a bit more, I realized that this demon was simply a harassing demon sent to afflict her in any way possible. It was not on her because of any sin of her own, or any generational curse, but was simply there to rob her of abundant life and fruitfulness for God. So knowing my authority in Christ, I simply took authority over this evil spirit and proclaimed the truth of the ownership of God over her body (much like a sheriff serving an eviction notice to illegal tenants on behalf of the legal owner). I cast off the afflicting spirit. Immediately she felt the pain leave her and was completely healed. This woman had been 'targeted' simply because she was hated by Satan and the demonic realm.

To understand effective ministry, we must embrace the old proverb 'Know thine enemy'. Obviously, the eyes of our heart are to be directed towards the person of God, not the person of Satan or his evil works. But the Christian who fails to take into account spiritual warfare in their overall perspective of living for Christ will continually be beset by problems. The will of God is that in the midst of the problems and trials that we will surely encounter we will be more than conquerors. To give one's life to Christ and to lay down one's life to serve him is to enlist in the army of God. As the Apostle Paul stated:

> *Our struggle is not against flesh and blood, but against the rulers, against the powers, against the world forces of this darkness, against the spiritual forces of wickedness in the heavenly places (Eph. 6:12).*

By 'heavenly places' Paul meant the spiritual realm.

The devil and his demonic minions will at times come against our lives as a 'roaring lion'. Peter wrote in 1 Peter 5:8:

> *Be of sober spirit, be on the alert. Your adversary, the devil, prowls around like a roaring lion, seeking someone to devour.*

As already discussed, when an individual practises sin there is an open door to the enemy in their life. However, there are times when a sickness is not due to sin or unbelief (or occurs after repentance of these issues), but simply to one's being a target of the enemy. Just as that sheriff evicting an illegal tenant knows that he has authority because of the badge issued to him, we must believe *and know* that we have authority as we represent Christ Jesus. That authority is exercised in the name of Jesus. As we represent him and his will, we carry a badge that the enemy can see even though we sometimes cannot. And the big guns that we can use against a resisting suspect are the gifts of the Holy Spirit. The ammunition we shoot from those guns is words and prayers of faith. Although we don't usually see things as they stand in the spiritual realm, the name of Jesus is the ultimate heat-seeking missile that always goes right to the target. This is why Jesus told the religious critics that if the demons were being cast off the people, the Kingdom of God had come near (Lk. 11: 20). When the presence and power of the King and of the Kingdom of God come near, the demonic hordes cannot remain. They will try to do so for a while if they think the representative of the Kingdom does not know his or her authority. The devil and his crew are liars. In fact, Satan is the father of lies. But when we are praying for the sick and the demonized, if we know our authority as Christ's ambassador and stand behind it in the name of Christ, the demons and their handiwork cannot remain.

Every fight, battle or war that has ever happened involves testing the emotional and physical strength and will of the opponent. You see this when wrestlers or boxers first enter the ring. They circle around each other and throw a few feints or jabs. They are not fighting in earnest – that comes later. They are merely sizing up the ability and will of their enemy. When it comes to long-term sickness and long delays to answered prayer, the enemy will often be throwing feints and jabs our way to try to size up our faith and if possible to discourage us. James 4:7b says, 'Resist the devil and he will flee from you.' Sometimes, however, that resistance takes quite a long time – even years. Is it that God is deaf, or unconcerned with us? No, quite the contrary. It's simply that he wants to use the situation we are in to help develop both Christlikeness and his specific will in our lives. When asked what we should be about, Jesus replied:

> *This is the work of God, that you believe in him whom he has sent (Jn. 6:29).*

We must continually remind ourselves that God is so very, very good, and that after giving us his Son, Jesus, there is absolutely nothing of value we need in our lives that he does not want to provide.

As John Eldredge has written in his excellent book, *Wild at Heart*, 'Life is not an ordeal to be survived, rather it is an adventure to be lived.' Persevering faith and prayers are about having long-term perspective. Loving and serving God in the midst of long-term disappointment and/or struggle is a definite art. All the saints of renown down through the ages have learnt this art. In a sense, it is learning to be content in God's love, no matter what circumstances we may find ourselves in. And just as with any epic adventure story, the breakthrough always comes after seemingly overwhelming odds and difficulties. It is the art of delighting ourselves in God and allowing him to bring about the very things he has purposed in our hearts. It is the Christlike art of saying no to self and preferring his will to ours. As Jesus stated:

> *Whenever a woman is in labour she has pain, because her hour has come; but when she gives birth to the child, she no longer remembers the anguish because of the joy that a child has been born into the world (Jn. 16:21).*

When the breakthrough or healing comes, the joy of victory makes light of the season of pain. Psalm 84:5–7 says:

> *How blessed is the man whose strength is in you, in whose heart are the highways to Zion! Passing through the valley of Baca they make it a spring; the early rain also covers it with blessings. They go from strength to strength, every one of them appears before God in Zion.*

Passing through the valley of Baca is symbolic of going through a dry, empty and difficult time in one's life. As a friend of mine says when referring to this passage, the word 'to' in going from 'strength to strength' should be spelt 'tooooooooooo', because it can seemingly last forever. It's the journey, however, that prepares us to walk in the fullness of the victory. It's the adventure, not merely the reward, that God uses to cause us to shine a bit more, like our heavenly Father – the Father of lights!

> *So I say to you, ask, and it will be given to you; seek, and you will find; knock, and it will be opened to you (Lk. 11:9).*

Chapter 9

Keeping Your Healing

MARC A. DUPONT

Put on the full armour of God, so that you will be able to stand firm against the schemes of the devil (Eph. 6:11).

The Apostle Paul's instruction in his second letter to Timothy, who was overseeing the church in Ephesus, was:

Guard, through the Holy Spirit who dwells in us, the treasure which has been entrusted to you (2 Tim. 1:14).

As noted in the previous chapter, humans have a fierce enemy who hates them deeply – the devil. According to Jesus, the devil is not only a liar, but the father of lies (Jn. 8:44). It follows, then, that as the creator of lying, he must be the all-time master of lying. He can be subtle, smooth and convincing. And often it seems he is far more aware of our weaknesses and insecurities than we are. He is adept at manipulating our vulnerabilities, like a maestro playing a violin. Without wanting to sound alarmist, this means we need to be on our guard constantly lest we fall prey to his tactics. In warning the church of Corinth about the devil and his evil tactics, the Apostle Paul wrote that 'even Satan disguises himself as an angel of light'.

Jesus stated that the 'thief', or the devil, came to steal, kill and destroy (Jn. 10:10). Specifically, he wants to rob us of what God has given us – the love, healing and provision of Christ and the Cross. Usually, he cannot by his own abilities actually take these things from us. When all is said and done, the Bible tells us we are more than conquerors in Christ Jesus and nothing can separate us from the love of God (Rom. 8:35–37). The Apostle John tells us that greater is he who is in us – the Holy Spirit, than he who is in the world – the devil (1 Jn. 4:4).

The great tool the devil can and does utilize against us, however, is lying. He often does so with great effectiveness. It is said that the greatest lie he ever told was that he did not exist. Most people who have given their lives to Christ Jesus understand that just as there is a reality to heaven, so there is also a reality to hell. Similarly, just as there is a reality to God, so there is also a reality to the devil. What many Christians fall prey to, however, is the thieving the devil does by lying about God's provision and healing in our lives. Specifically, while a Christian can know they are heaven-bound thanks to the Cross, when it comes to the hope of good relationships, healing, financial provision and destiny here on earth there can be a real lack of faith due to the continual warfare of the devil's lies. A prevailing 'spirit', or mindset, of poverty can rob many not only of what God intends for them to come into, but also of the very breakthroughs they have already experienced. For example, with many there is a prevailing fear that what they have they will surely lose – as if the success, blessings or breakthroughs they have experienced with God are some sort of fluke. And when God does happen to bless us in a certain area of our life, the lie will continue that he probably won't want to meet any of the other needs of my life, etc, etc.

Completely contrary to all of these false reasonings are the Bible's promises of God's faithfulness, such as James 1:17, which says:

Every good thing given and every perfect gift is from above, coming down from the Father of lights, with whom there is no variation or shifting shadow.

The implications of this passage are rich for two reasons. First, James echoes the promise which runs consistently through the Bible – that God is Jehovah Jirah, the Lord God who provides for all of our needs. Secondly, and equally importantly, he states the truth that God is never capricious, whimsical or inconsistent, as we often are when it comes to commitments.

I recently read a testimonial book published by a Californian church in which I have done a lot of ministry since its foundation. One of the remarkable stories concerned a lady who was healed of a serious foot injury she had lived with for over twenty years. She had given her life to Christ some years before the actual healing took place. It happened while I was ministering in the church in 2004. Although the woman absolutely knew God loved her, she never dreamed he would want to heal her foot. The bones of her foot had healed incorrectly because she had refused to go to a doctor following her accident.

When the healing took place she was overwhelmed with joy and surprise, first because the injury was, in effect, very much a disability. She was unable to walk without extreme pain. When the Lord healed her, she was so completely healed that she could even run again for the first time in over two decades. Secondly, she was deeply blessed because she had never dreamed the Lord would actually want to heal her.

She had been directed by the Lord to do something during the meeting which she felt very uncomfortable doing. What the Lord led her to do was nothing very embarrassing or demeaning; it was just outside her personal comfort zone. As one of the two senior pastors of that particular church likes to say, 'God is everywhere in the universe, except for one area – your personal comfort zone.' But as a result of her obedience, and to her great surprise, the Lord performed a miracle. According to her testimony, she had felt that her damaged foot was simply the cross she was to carry for her reckless lifestyle prior to coming to Christ. She had never even thought of asking the Lord to heal her. As the Apostle James also wrote, we do not have, because we do not ask (Jas. 4:2).

The thief of belief

A secondary way in which Satan robs many who lack belief in the goodness of God is through the fear that God won't allow us to keep what he's given us. I'm not speaking here about money, houses or cars. Where material blessings are concerned we are merely stewards, entrusted by God with his provision for the Kingdom of God. With the personal victories and healings that the Lord has wrought in our lives, however, all too often some cannot hang on to what God has delighted in doing for them.

Allow me to give an illustration. Perhaps you gave your life to Christ in a Sunday morning service when the pastor gave an altar call for salvation. Or possibly it was in a Billy Graham type of outreach and you went forward to pray the 'sinner's prayer' of salvation. Or perhaps it was simply as a result of a friend sharing the Gospel with you and then praying with you. Almost all who do so experience that 'still small voice' in their heart of hearts, i.e. their spirit.

This revelation of God's love is, at least in the beginning of our walk with God, how we know we are saved. Many have a profound initial salvation experience. Whether it's 'deep calling to deep' or the fire of God's holiness that touches one's heart, there is always a true and discernible touch of God.

During the ensuing days or weeks, however, many also experience Satan's onslaught of lies. They go something like this: 'You didn't really experience God – what you had was just an emotional experience,' or, 'Well, maybe other people were saved, but God couldn't possibly love you – look at how insignificant you are,' or again, 'You simply have sinned too much – there's no forgiveness for you!' One day you know you've experienced the life-changing love of God, and the next you feel completely abandoned. What you were experiencing at that precise point in time is called 'spiritual warfare'. The hater of your soul – the devil, who came to steal, kill and destroy – is employing the greatest weapon in his arsenal. He is lying to you in an attempt to rob you of your faith in God and in his goodness towards you.

Snakes in the grass

If you can understand that as God's created children you are deeply hated by the sworn enemy of God, you can begin to understand that he will use any tactic he can to get into your head and rob you of the love God has for you in Christ Jesus. And, as we've examined throughout this book, a very large part of God's love is expressed in the healing he performs in our bodies and souls. After all, Jesus came to destroy the works of the devil. So if the devil cannot prevent you coming to Christ, he most certainly will attempt to prevent you from coming into the blessings God has for you. And if he cannot prevent you from coming into those blessings, he will attempt to rob you of them once you have them.

The first instance of Satan attempting to destroy or rob a human was when he came as a serpent to Eve in the Garden. The first words from his mouth were, 'Did God really say ... ?' The whole fall of humanity from intimacy with God can be directly traced to the devil deceiving it with a lie. And that lie is the same today: 'God really doesn't want to give you his best. He's keeping from you what you need the most.' It was for solid reasons that thousands of years later both Jesus and John the Baptist referred to hypocritical religious leaders of their day as 'snakes'. Today, too, there are religious leaders who promote unbelief in God's goodness towards you and me. The lie is the same every time – that God is either unwilling or unable to show kindness to you and me in a very personal way. And just as a snake slithers with great subtlety through the grass, so the lies of the devil come to us very subtly through the grid of our minds.

There are two basic ways in which the devil will try to rob you of a healing or other blessing that God has already given you. First, as we've seen, the devil is a liar, and so just as he came to you with a lie concerning your initial salvation experience, so, in turn, he will attempt to lie to you concerning a healing you may have received. Secondly, if the illness or symptoms you were experiencing were due to unhealthy behaviour and/or sin, the devil will tempt you to fall back into old patterns of destructive behaviour, with the result that the symptoms return.

As we've already mentioned, sometimes when God heals it is instantaneous. Sometimes, however, it is not. Healing can sometimes be a process in which the recipient rejoices over each stage of healing, but needs to continue to exercise faith for the whole healing. Luke, the beloved physician, relates the following story in his Gospel:

> *As he [Jesus] entered a village, ten leprous men who stood at a distance met him; and they raised their voices, saying, 'Jesus, Master, have mercy on us!' When he saw them, he said to them, 'Go and show yourselves to the priests.' And as they were going, they were cleansed (Lk. 17:12–14).*

In this particular case, the healing itself was conditional on their obedience to Jesus. It is often the same today.

Unfortunately, there are cases in which although people are partially, and sometimes even completely, healed, they lose their healing because of their unbelief. I recently read an interview with an internationally known politician who had lost a national election, who said, 'We did not lose; rather my opponent won'! We live in an age in which we rationalize situations from a highly subjective and sometimes self-centred perspective. Our current pop sociological thinking necessitates that questions pertaining to truth be qualified as to what *type* of truth – objective truth, subjective truth, general truth or specific limited truth – which makes us look good no matter how serious the failure. We are the society which coined the phrase 'putting a spin' on the truth.

The truth concerning the Kingdom of God, however, is always the same, because God is the same yesterday, today and forever. The good news is that Jesus is very much present, and he is good all the time. With him there is no selfishness, turning or shadows. The Cross has bridged the gap between an all-powerful and benevolent Creator and the sinful creation he loves. The battle really lies not with God, but with us – in our minds and hearts.

As we've said, our God is neither capricious nor whimsical. He has given us the gift of his only begotten Son, Jesus, and there is no other need we may have that compares with what he has already given us. In this blood covenant, or promise of faithfulness, there is provision for healing. The prophet Isaiah stated:

> *He was pierced through for our transgressions, he was crushed for our iniquities; the chastening for our well-being fell upon him, and by his scourging we are healed (Is. 53:5).*

Faith based on presumption is one thing. It is a mistake to claim God has done something when he clearly has not. Sometimes it takes more faith to admit there is a problem and come to God with the reality of that problem than it takes to hide our heads in the sand like an ostrich, hoping it will simply go away. Having said that, however, we must not shrink back in faith when we actually know that God has brought about a level of healing or blessing.

Often we can fight a real faith battle against all odds and dare to believe God has the best for us, only to lose the fight when the healing or goal is within reach. Like a boxer who has scored more points than his opponent over the first fourteen rounds but relaxes his guard so much that he's knocked out in the fifteenth, we can relax and fall prey to the deceits of the enemy. This is one of the primary reasons why some who have the faith to get prayer for their physical problem experience a bit of healing but end up losing it. I have even seen a few cases where the symptoms disappear completely, only for the person to reopen the door to the enemy through fear which is rooted in unbelief. We must constantly remember that we not only step into eternal life through faith, but we are also called to walk daily in faith – faith in God and his constant care and provision for our lives.

Go and sin no more

John 5 contains one of the classic stories of healing in the Gospels. It is the story of Jesus walking up to a man at the Pool of Bethesda who had been lame for thirty-eight years. Jesus performed a miracle and healed his leg. Some time later on the same day, Jesus encountered the man at the Temple. Jesus said to him:

> *Behold, you have become well; do not sin any more, so that nothing worse happens to you (Jn. 5:14).*

While some physical ailments are the result of sin in the life of the sick or ailing individual, many illnesses are not due to sin. It is often a mistake to tell someone their sickness is due to sin, unless you know the person well and can speak with a pastor's heart, or you have a proven track record of hearing from God and can communicate that truth with a father's heart. I strongly recommend that you do not say anything like this to people you are praying for unless you have been given that sort of authority by a pastor who has monitored your track record of fruitfulness in ministry. Sadly, however, there are people who have opened the door to ill health by practising sin in their life. This can happen both directly and indirectly: directly, as with an alcoholic who develops cirrhosis of the liver by constant alcohol abuse, or indirectly, as with a user of pornography who opens the door to afflicting spirits. Sin is Satan's legal territory, and when sin is cumulative, big doors are opened up.

In the type of situations mentioned in the previous paragraph God can, and often does, bring temporary healing to the physical symptoms resulting from the behaviour. But to keep the healing, the behaviour which brought about the problem must be stopped. The door opened to the enemy must be closed. That is to say, one must turn from unrighteous behaviour to righteous behaviour, or in other words, from unhealthy behaviour to healthy behaviour. This essentially is the biblical definition of repentance.

God is God! He is a God of incredible mercy and grace. His loving kindness for us has no parallel. But in the midst of all the healing and blessings he has for us he is still very much God, and that means he demands that we learn to walk in his ways if we would walk in his love and care. He is not like a small retail shop where we can run in and grab some chips and a coke, but leave the milk and cereal on the shelf. It's either all or nothing with him, simply because he is God. Often he releases healing and other blessings in degrees to our lives because he wants to test the faithfulness of our hearts, as in the story of the ten men with leprosy. All were healed, but only one returned to Jesus to thank him. Jesus said to the man:

> *'Were there not ten cleansed? But the nine – where are they? Was no one found who returned to give glory to God, except this foreigner?' And he said to him, 'Stand up and go; your faith has made you well' (Lk. 17:17–19).*

Although all were healed of their skin condition, only one of them walked away with the fullness of what God had for him.

If you yourself have in the past experienced a degree of healing or victory, only to have all the symptoms and/or problems return, don't lose heart. As discouraging as the return of the difficulties may be, know deep in your heart that God is always for you. And if in reading this you know you have faith in God's love for you but find it hard to believe that he wants to heal you, please take to heart the words of Jesus found in Matthew 17:20 concerning serious troubles and trials:

Truly I say to you, if you have faith the size of a mustard seed, you will say to this mountain, 'Move from here to there,' and it will move; and nothing will be impossible to you.

In the culture of that day the word mountain was often used as a metaphor for great difficulties. The good news is we don't need a mountain of faith to move a mustard seed. If we just keep seeking God and believing that he does have his very best for us, we will come into it.

Also, if your symptoms of a serious problem have come back and you know it's due to unrighteous practices, repent. God is not one to quickly lose heart. He is long-suffering and quick to forgive and restore when we are honest with him and turn to walk in his love and truth.

God is good, and, as they respond in much of Africa, 'all the time'. His good will and intentions are working in our lives even when we don't sense his nearness and purposes. He is very aware of our frailties and vulnerabilities. Psalm 103:13–14 says:

Just as a father has compassion on his children, so the LORD *has compassion on those who fear him. For he himself knows our frame; he is mindful that we are but dust.*

And finally, in the words of Isaiah the prophet:

Therefore the LORD longs to be gracious to you,
And therefore He waits on high to have compassion
 on you.
For the LORD is a God of justice;
How blessed are all those who long for Him

(Is. 30:18)

Chapter 10

Ministering to the Lost

MARK STIBBE

Two years ago I was in my local newsagent's buying a newspaper. As I looked for my paper, my eyes wandered to the magazines just above the broadsheets and I saw a copy of the latest *Reader's Digest* journal. This was for the month of September 2002. The front cover displayed a statement concerning what doctors now know about the healing power of faith. Intrigued, I bought the magazine and went home and read it. The main article contained the following statement:

> Scientific studies correlating faith with good health are starting to convert a sceptical medical community. It's all part of a general revival of interest in spirituality. Three quarters of British people say they are aware of a spiritual dimension to their lives.

Research accumulated in the article demonstrated how scientists have made five important discoveries about the relationship between religious faith (of whatever kind) and good health:

- Those who attend church live longer
- Believers have a better post-op recovery rate

- Prayer reduces the chances of heart disease

- Religion protects you against high blood pressure

- More prayer means less stress and depression

The importance of these findings should not be under-estimated. While the *Reader's Digest* did not take an exclusively Christian perspective on faith and health, the article does reflect a growing openness in western culture to the relationship between prayer and healing. The truth is, many people, whether Christian or not, are very open to being prayed for when they are sick or have some other kind of need. There is in fact a greater receptivity to spiritual healing than there has been in a very long time. A door of opportunity for praying for the sick is open at the beginning of the twenty-first century.

In my introduction to this book I quoted Raymond Fung (until recently the secretary of evangelism at the World Council of Churches), who wrote, 'Quantitatively the number one means of evangelism today, of people coming to faith in Jesus Christ, is probably … healing.' As far as the west is concerned, this statement needs to be put in the context of the move from modernism (with its emphasis on scientific rationality) to postmodernism (with its emphasis on experience, even mystical experience). Whereas in the modernist era it was unfashionable to talk about the spiritual dimension of life, today the opposite is true. Indeed, it is possible to say that whereas forty years ago the average westerner was an example of *homo materialis* (materialistic man), today he or she is much more likely to be an example of *homo spiritualis* (spiritual man). The downside of this greater spiritual openness is of course that people today seem to be prepared to believe almost any religious view, however absurd. The upside is that at last much of western culture is receptive to a more experiential spirituality. In such a context, the Christian ministry of divine healing can make significant inroads.

There can be miracles

On one of my most recent trips to the USA, I was waiting in an airport lounge so I picked up a magazine next to me. In it there was an article on the Hollywood superstar Sharon Stone. The interviewer was particularly interested in finding out how Stone had coped during a time when she had experienced severe problems with her health and her marriage. She replied, 'What I have to say is that I've always been a spiritual person. The one thing that has remained very consistent in my life during this time off is my faith. It's clear to me that God has a plan and a purpose for me. I walk in the joy and the ease of that.' Stone elaborated by saying that she was now into spiritual healing, particularly 'Reiki healing'. In fact, the press reported how she had prayed for a man in a shop who had experienced healing. She had this to say:

> I don't know if I saved his life or if he just got better. He had cancer in his face. I won't disrespect his privacy by discussing the intimacies of his situation with you. But I will say that I did healing work with him. He believes that this is the reason that his cancer went away. I am incredibly grateful that his cancer is in remission. I'm a person who doesn't just believe in miracles. I count on them as a way of life.

Now that last comment is important. While Christian readers will want to question Reiki healing, there is great significance in Stone's comment about believing in and counting on miracles. She is not alone in that. In fact, I sometimes think there is more faith outside the church than there is inside it! My experience of praying for non-Christians is that they really do have faith in God's power to heal. I remember one time flying with a team to Scandinavia and discovering that one of the female flight attendants (not a Christian) had such a serious condition in both her legs that she had to wear trousers rather than a skirt. One of my team was herself a flight attendant and approached the lady about her and me praying for her when the plane had landed. She said that she would love that, so we waited until we arrived at our destination. Once everyone had left the plane, she phoned the captain and said to him, 'I'll be a few minutes late getting off the plane. I'm about to receive some healing.'

'I'm about to receive some healing.' What a statement! How many times have you heard a *Christian* say that before receiving healing prayer? Not often, I suspect. This lady had real faith that something would happen, and it did. The Holy Spirit powerfully touched her, and even though we never heard the full extent of the healing, we know she received some, as she said she would. Even more encouraging was the comment made by her fellow flight attendant, a very confident lady who asked whether we had been praying for healing. I said yes and then asked if she believed in God's power to heal. She replied that she had not until three weeks before. She then told me the following:

Three weeks ago I woke up with a stiff neck. It was so painful, I could not move my head to the left or the right and I realized that I wouldn't be able to go to work. I came downstairs to the breakfast table. I share a house with a Christian girl who believes in healing. She asked whether she could pray for me. I wasn't at all into this sort of thing but because it was so painful I said yes. She gently laid hands on my neck and prayed out loud. Immediately I felt this heat on my neck and within seconds I was completely healed. If you'd asked me four weeks ago whether I believed in what you've just been doing, I would almost certainly have said no. But I really believe it now.

Needless to say, her experience opened up a great opportunity to witness about Jesus.

The point I want to stress is this. There is a door open to believers right now to take the ministry of divine healing out of the four walls of the church and into the streets, schools, pubs, workplaces, trains, planes and automobiles of our nation. People really are very receptive to being prayed for, and they are far more open than ever to the possibility of miracles occurring. The secular humanism and scientific rationalism of the modernist era have been tried and found wanting. The myth of scientific progress did not deliver a better world. In fact, it gave us horrific world wars, one of which culminated in the use of the atom bomb. While science and reason are still vital in postmodernity, they are no longer seen as the only ways of understanding reality. Experience, intuition, emotion, mysticism and miracles have a place too. In a culture that believes 'there can be miracles', it would be a wasted opportunity if the church either neglected the ministry of divine healing or confined it to believers alone. If we fail to minister healing in Jesus' name to seekers, they will start looking in other places – some of them decidedly dubious and even dangerous – for the health and wholeness that they need. It really is time for the church to rise up and to use gifts like healing and prophecy on the streets.

Learning from Jesus

Whenever I teach on the subject of ministering divine healing to the lost, I begin by looking at one particular story in the ministry of Jesus. Actually, one could take pretty well any of the healing miracles of Jesus as the starting point for a discussion about ministering healing to the lost. We tend to forget that none of the people who received healing from Jesus were disciples. None of them had been born again, not least because Jesus had not yet died for their sins. Neither were they fully signed up members of local churches, because churches did not exist until after Pentecost. No, Jesus ministered healing to the lost, not the saved. Out of his great compassion he shared the Father's love with people who had not yet said 'yes' to the call to follow him. As Matthew reports in chapter 9 of his Gospel:

Jesus travelled through all the cities and villages of that area, teaching in the synagogues and announcing the Good News about the Kingdom. And wherever he went, he healed people of every sort of disease and illness. He felt great pity for the crowds that came, because their problems were so great and they didn't know where to go for help. They were like sheep without a shepherd (Mt. 9:35–36).

While most of the healing miracles of Jesus could serve as a great starting point for learning how to minister healing to the lost, one has always struck me as particularly insightful: the healing of blind Bartimaeus. Mark records this incident in chapter 10 of his Gospel:

And so they reached Jericho. Later, as Jesus and his disciples left town, a great crowd was following. A blind beggar named Bartimaeus (son of Timaeus) was sitting beside the road as Jesus was going by. When Bartimaeus heard that Jesus from Nazareth was nearby, he began to shout out, 'Jesus, Son of David, have mercy on me!'

'Be quiet!' some of the people yelled at him But he only shouted louder, 'Son of David, have mercy on me!'

> *When Jesus heard him, he stopped and said, 'Tell him to come here.'*
>
> *So they called the blind man. 'Cheer up,' they said. 'Come on, he's calling you!' Bartimaeus threw aside his coat, jumped up, and came to Jesus.*
>
> *'What do you want me to do for you?' Jesus asked.*
>
> *'Teacher,' the blind man said, 'I want to see!'*
>
> *And Jesus said to him, 'Go your way. Your faith has healed you.' And instantly the blind man could see! Then he followed Jesus down the road* (Mk. 10:46–52).

One vital thing to remember right at the outset is that in this incident Jesus heals someone who was not at the time a follower of his. At the beginning of the story Mark says that Bartimaeus was sitting by the roadside. The word translated 'roadside' is the Greek word *hodos*, meaning 'way'. In Mark's Gospel, the word 'way' is a metaphor pointing to the road the disciple must walk. The earliest Christians were in fact called 'the People of the Way'. At the start of the story, Bartimaeus is 'by the way', not 'on the way'. To be sure, he hears the call of Jesus (literally) and jumps up, comes to Jesus and leaves his cloak – the symbol of his former way of life – behind him (much as the fishermen leave their nets in Luke 5:11). But it is not until *after* he has been healed of his blindness that, Mark says, Bartimaeus followed Jesus down the road. The word 'road' here is again the word *hodos*. After receiving healing from Jesus, Bartimaeus follows him 'on the way'. But at the time of receiving his healing, Bartimaeus was not yet a disciple. He had not yet said yes to the call to discipleship. All he was responding to was the possibility that Jesus of Nazareth could heal him. For this Jesus applauds him, saying, 'Go your way. Your faith has healed you.' Having been invited to go his own way, Bartimaeus freely chooses to go Jesus' way.

This then is a magnificent illustration of Jesus' healing ministry to the lost – of how to use divine healing in evangelism. From it I want to draw out four practical lessons about ministering healing outside the church.

1. *Always be ready to act*

Notice how Mark begins his account of the healing of blind Bartimaeus:

And so they reached Jericho. Later, as Jesus and his disciples left town, a great crowd was following. A blind beggar named Bartimaeus (son of Timaeus) was sitting beside the road as Jesus was going by.

One of the things you learn in theology degree courses is the way in which the storytellers of the Bible often leave what are called 'gaps' in their narratives. In modern novels there is of course a great deal of detail. The storytellers seek to provide as much information as possible, sometimes to the point of tedium. With biblical narratives it is altogether different. The Gospels, for example, contain many gaps. Their narrators do not seek to fill in every gap in our knowledge as readers. They work by what is called 'artful reticence'. By their silence in certain matters they actually provoke the reader into greater imaginative exploration.

Here is a really good example of that. Look at what Mark's narrator does. He tells us first of all that Jesus and his disciples came to Jericho. Jericho was a great city and we know from Luke's Gospel that Jesus did some amazing ministry there. The call of Zacchaeus, for example, happens as Jesus travels through Jericho. But Mark does not mention any of this. No sooner has he said that they came to Jericho than, in the next breath, he is reporting something that occurred as they were leaving.

What an enormous gap! What happened between them arriving and them leaving? Didn't Mark want to report any of the teaching or the actions of Jesus in the city itself? What is going on here?

This is an instance where a deliberate 'gap' creates a point of major significance. The truth is, Jesus' mission in Jericho was no doubt very powerful. He no doubt gave some great messages and performed some great miracles. At the same time, the most spectacular and memorable thing of all happened after the mission outside the city, not during the mission inside the city. Now this is supremely important. Many Christians today invest in missions and conferences. They come to both with a greater level of faith and expectancy than they ever do in the more humdrum and ongoing life of their local churches, let alone on the streets of their towns and cities. In the larger contexts, amidst the crowds, they often hear great teaching and see great miracles. But then, as soon as the auditorium empties and the people go home, that same faith is somehow switched off with the stage lights. Outside the conference, on the way home, they no longer expect the great things they looked for when they were in the meetings.

When Mark chooses to omit what happened in Jericho, and go straight from when they reached Jericho to when they left town, he is actually sending a very strong signal to Christians such as this. He is saying that we can see miracles outside the big settings in unexpected places. Indeed, he is saying that we should *expect* to see great things outside our meetings and our missions. The most memorable miracle of the Jericho mission happened outside the city when it was all over, not in the city while it was all happening. On the road out of Jericho, a blind man was miraculously healed. Even the name of the man is remembered – Bartimaeus, that is, the son of Timaeus – and that is certainly unusual in the Gospel healing miracles.

If that doesn't tell us how memorable this miracle was, nothing will.

The first point I want to make is this: **always be ready to act**. Do not confine your expectation of God's healing power to the worship place. Expect him to move in the workplace too. Don't restrict your faith to the nave. Expect God to move in power in the neighbourhood as well. As John Wimber used to say, 'The meat is on the streets.'

Part of our problem is that we still operate with the Greek, dualistic mindset that says that the sacred places are where God lives, whereas the mundane places are too profane for God. That is a lie. The Hebraic mindset is totally different from the Hellenistic or Greek way of thinking. To the Hebrew mindset – the mindset of the biblical authors – 'The earth is the Lord's and everything in it.' The whole of creation is the Lord's. God has access anywhere and everywhere. Indeed he is omnipresent in creation (while not being the same as creation). That is why King David can exclaim in Psalm 139:

> *I can never escape from your spirit!*
> *I can never get away from your presence!*
> *If I go up to heaven, you are there;*
> *if I go down to the place of the dead, you are there.*
> *If I ride the wings of the morning,*
> *if I dwell by the farthest oceans,*
> *even there your hand will guide me,*
> *and your strength will support me* (Ps. 139:7–10).

God's Spirit and his presence are everywhere. Jesus knew that. So he did not restrict his mighty works to the religious places – like the Temple or the synagogues – but he ministered in mighty power everywhere.

Those who want to minister divine healing to the lost must operate with Jesus' worldview. They must renounce the old Greek mindset that causes us to switch off to the

God dimension as soon as we are outside the church meeting or the conference setting. They must allow God's power to demolish that wrong stronghold that the enemy has over their thinking and start believing that God can perform mighty works anywhere, any time. This more integrated way of thinking is absolutely critical for an effective ministry of healing to the lost. We cannot begin to be used in this way until we are always prepared to act, whenever or wherever the need arises.

One couple who have really understood this are Bob and Sue Brassett. Recently they were on their way to a healing conference at Toronto Airport Christian Fellowship. This is what occurred on the plane:

The healings actually began on our plane trip there. The jet became a healing room. About two hours into our 4½-hour flight from Victoria, BC, to Toronto, something happened. A voice came over the PA, 'Is there a doctor present on the flight? We have a medical emergency.' After about 20–30 minutes or so, I got up to go to the rest room. Sue said, 'Find out, if you can, what the medical emergency is.' As I proceeded toward the rear of the plane, I noticed an older lady quietly weeping. I leaned over and said, 'Excuse me, but I am a minister. Was it your husband who had the medical emergency?'

She said, 'Yes, the doctor thinks it's a stroke and he also has Alzheimer's.' I asked her if I could pray with her. 'Oh yes, please,' she replied. I sat down next to her. She told me that he had also had a sudden worsening of his Alzheimer's, and then what appeared to be a stroke. She told me that although her husband had been a pastor for over forty years, she didn't particularly believe in healing.

I said, 'That's OK, I have enough faith for us both. Let's pray.' I spoke blessing and healing and rebuked the cause and effect of Alzheimer's and a Cerebral Vascular Accident. At the very moment I said 'amen', the flight attendant came to the seat saying, 'Excuse me, ma'am, I have good news. Just moments ago, your husband suddenly returned to normal. The doctor doesn't understand it, but he seems to be just fine!'

The woman expressed great joy and thankfulness and then she said, 'My stomach pain is gone! I think I'm healed also! I'll have my breakfast now that I couldn't eat earlier.'

Upon returning to my seat, the man sitting next to me asked what happened. I told him about the healing of the husband and wife. 'Well, I'm not a Christian,' he said. 'In fact, I've never been in a church in my entire life. But I have severe migraine headaches. Do you think God would heal me if you prayed?'

I replied, 'Yes.' He told me the headaches were triggered by cheese, chocolate or red wine. When I finished praying, my wife Sue leaned over and, not knowing of the prayer or his medical condition, asked if I would like a chocolate. She then offered one to the gentleman as well.

'OK,' he said, 'I'm willing to test out if I'm healed. I'll eat the chocolate.'

He did and experienced no problem or pain throughout the entire rest of the flight. Then we had an opportunity to pray with the flight attendant.

Why were Bob and Sue used so powerfully in this story? The simple answer is because they were 'always ready to act'. They did not expect God to restrict his healings to the conference time and the conference place. They had an expectation that God would move outside and beyond such environments. Like Jesus, who was ready to act outside Jericho after the mission, Bob and Sue were ready to act on a plane before the conference had begun. Those who want to minister healing to the lost must always be prepared to act, wherever or whenever the Holy Spirit leads.

2. *Always be ready to listen*

If we return to Mark's narrative of the healing of blind
Bartimaeus, the second important lesson concerns being
attentive to the cries of the lost all around us. When
Bartimaeus learnt that Jesus of Nazareth was about to
pass by, he started shouting very loudly. This is how Mark
reports the incident:

> *When Bartimaeus heard that Jesus from Nazareth was nearby, he*
> *began to shout out, 'Jesus, Son of David, have mercy on me!'*
> *'Be quiet!' some of the people yelled at him But he only shouted*
> *louder, 'Son of David, have mercy on me!'*

The commentators make much of the content of
Bartimaeus' words here, showing how his confession of
Jesus as 'Son of David' reveals an understanding of Jesus
that is ironically full of spiritual sight for one physically
blind. But it is not just what Bartimaeus says but how he
says it, and how many times he says it. Mark writes that
Bartimaeus shouted out to Jesus and that people in the
crowd told him to shut up. Bartimaeus was desperate,
however, so he shouted all the more.

One of the most important lessons for us to learn in
ministering healing to the lost is to be attentive to the cries
(both vocalized and hidden) of those who do not know
Christ. More than that, when we actually hear those cries,
the important thing is not to ignore or suppress them but
to attend to them. If the first key value in ministering
healing to the lost is 'always be ready to act', the second
is **always be ready to listen**. Instead of being indifferent
to the world's lament, we must become compassionately
and consistently attentive.

I remember speaking at a conference in the UK. In the
afternoon I conducted a workshop for church leaders.
There were about forty of them and the subject was how

to develop a vision for your church. Much of what I was saying was born out of my own experience leading St Andrew's Chorleywood, where we have a vision that is very focused on sharing the Father's love with those who do not know Jesus, especially in our local community. I was emphasizing to the leaders that the seasons have changed and that we have now entered a time-frame in which local churches have a great window of opportunity in evangelism. I told the group that if they developed a vision for ministering to the lost in their communities, God would certainly honour that in due course.

At that moment the doors at the back of the church building suddenly crashed open and a drunken man walked in. He listened for a moment to what I was saying and then shouted from the back of the church the words, 'Sir, sir, I need God!' Clearly I was in a dilemma. Here I was talking about opening the doors of your church to the lost in a leaders' seminar, and now a lost man had entered the building! Responding as quickly as I could, I sent two of my team to the back to minister to the man. After two minutes, however, the man broke free and shouted even louder, this time only a few feet away from me, 'Sir, sir, I need God!' At that moment I couldn't avoid hearing what he had to say, nor could anyone else. Some of the leaders looked very angry and, I think, had they had the opportunity, would have done what the crowd did with Bartimaeus: rebuked him! Some of them were especially unhappy when I dismissed the leaders early in order to spend time listening to the man's story and pray for him. But that is what happened. They left, and we heard the man's story.

And what a painful story it was. He had been a soldier in the British Army during the first Gulf War in the early 1990s. He had killed enemy soldiers in action and had been trying to drown his guilt in alcohol ever since. That afternoon he had been walking past the church and had suddenly felt that he had to go in. We talked to him about the Cross, and about the pardon and peace that could be his if he repented and turned to Jesus. He did that there and then, received Jesus Christ into his heart as Saviour, and was clearly touched by the Holy Spirit. We prayed for deliverance from his alcohol addiction and he seemed utterly freed and changed after that. He left the church later, after tea and sandwiches with the leaders, a completely new person. So, **always be ready to listen**!

There is an interesting twist to this story. About six months later I was preaching at the national Elim Pentecostal conference in Wales. I told this story in the morning Bible reading on Thursday, and then on the Thursday evening I preached my final message. As I did so, a drunken man from the local town wandered in shouting, 'What this man is saying is really helpful.'

Aside from this being one of the greatest compliments to my preaching I have ever received, the incident put me in a quandary. I had shared the story in the morning about how I had dismissed the leaders when a drunken man had entered my meeting before. I had emphasized the importance of always being ready to listen to the needs of the lost. Now, that very evening, in the presence of hundreds who had heard me in the morning, I was being confronted yet again by exactly the same scenario. At the same time, I also knew that I had to preach the message that night. In fact, I had thrown away my notes and was in the middle of an unprepared talk. So I stopped proceedings while two leaders escorted the man out of the hall and I asked everyone to join with me in praying for the man. This we did, asking God to meet him outside the hall, and to speak powerfully to him.

A few weeks later I had a letter from a pastor who had been at the morning meeting but had been playing with his son during the evening meeting that was interrupted. He wrote:

> I'm an associate pastor at an Elim Church (Church on the Way). You talked about taking God out of the meetings. Me and my son were playing frisbee near our chalet. The wind took the frisbee right over the fence. I went to find it but just as I was about to give up, I saw someone on the other side of the road. Guess who? It was the same man who had interrupted your testimony in Lunars, when you were talking about the Father's love. We got talking and I prayed for him. He began to weep a bit, but I just know God has plans for him.

That is truly remarkable. We prayed in the meeting that God would meet with the man outside the hall. A pastor was playing frisbee with his son, and the frisbee caught the wind and brought him face to face with the man we had been praying for. As that happened, the pastor was given an opportunity to minister to the man. Talk about answered prayer!

I believe that we need to become more attentive to the needs of the lost around us. So much of our churches' life is geared towards those who are already members. But the church exists to welcome those who are not yet members. For us to become effective in reaching out to such as these, we will need not only to be always ready to act, but also to be always ready to listen. Compassionate, selfless attention to the needs of those who are far away from God is what is required. This means not rebuking those, like Bartimaeus, who cause glorious disorder, but rather embracing them.

3. *Always be ready to stop*

Returning to the story, we read how Jesus responded to the insistent cries of the blind man by the road:

When Jesus heard him, he stopped and said, 'Tell him to come here.'

So they called the blind man. 'Cheer up,' they said. 'Come on, he's calling you!' Bartimaeus threw aside his coat, jumped up, and came to Jesus.

There was a time when my favourite verse in the Bible was the two words in John 11:35, 'Jesus wept'. There is a wealth of theology in those two words. If Jesus shows us the Father, then the weeping (literally 'sobbing') of Jesus at Lazarus' tomb provides us with an absolutely unique understanding of the nature of God. It reveals that God is not remote from human suffering but involved in it. It shows that God weeps when we weep. He is not the apathetic, detached and unmovable deity of the ancient Greeks. He is the perfect, compassionate Dad who feels what we feel. Truly, the two words 'Jesus wept' are utterly remarkable.

At the same time, I have to confess that in recent days these two words have been superseded by the two words that Mark writes here in the story of blind Bartimaeus. When Mark writes that Jesus 'stopped' (literally, 'stopped still in his tracks'), I marvel even more. Jesus was leading a crowd out of Jericho, but he stopped the whole crowd for just one man.

We have seen this kind of extravagant compassion already in Mark's Gospel. If you track back to Mark chapter 4 you will find Jesus crossing the Sea of Galilee in a great storm. He stills the storm and then he and his disciples arrive at the pagan side of the lake, in the region of the Decapolis. At the beginning of chapter 5, Mark reports:

So they arrived at the other side of the lake, in the land of the Gerasenes. Just as Jesus was climbing from the boat, a man possessed by an evil spirit ran out from a cemetery to meet him (Mk. 5:1–2).

What follows, over the next eighteen verses, is an extra-ordinary and indeed lengthy encounter between Jesus and a severely demonized man. He has just crossed the sea and confronted great dangers. Now he has arrived on the other side and he is confronted by great demons. This is truly going from the frying pan into the fire, as the saying goes. Yet the important thing to note is that Jesus spends time attending to the man's needs. He stops and interacts with the man before delivering him of his demons by casting them into two thousand pigs. These pigs – worth several hundreds of thousands of pounds in today's money – then run into the sea and drown.

The story teaches one lesson powerfully: Jesus crossed a lake to minister to just one man. He stopped on the shores in order to set one person free. He does not go anywhere other than the shore. As soon as he has set the man free, Jesus and his disciples cross back to the Jewish side of the lake. On returning, Jesus starts walking with his disciples to the house of a local synagogue leader called Jairus. Jairus has begged Jesus to come and heal his twelve-year-old daughter, who is dying. En route to their destination, a woman who has been suffering a bleeding disorder for twelve years pushes past the people behind Jesus and reaches out to touch him. Immediately Jesus stops the crowd, turns round, and seeks the one who has touched him. He stops a whole crowd for just one person! Truly, Jesus' ministry reveals the value of just one human life.

Accordingly, the third vital lesson for ministering healing to the lost is this: **always be ready to stop**. The truth is that the pace of life for most of us is unhealthily fast. As long ago as 1949, these anonymous verses were printed in a national newspaper:

Time of the Mad Atom

This is the age
Of the half-read page.
And the quick hash
And the mad dash.
The bright night
With the nerves tight.
The plane hop
With the brief stop.
The lamp tan
In a short span.
The Big Shot
In a good spot.
And the brain strain,
The heart pain.
And the cat naps
Till the spring snaps –

And the fun's done!

That was 1949! It is a lot worse today. Too many of us suffer from what psychologists call 'hurry sickness'. In such a mad dash, too few have the time or the motivation to stop in order to help someone else in real need. Too many hurry on by.

The example of Jesus in Mark 10, and indeed in the rest of the Gospels, highlights the importance of the following life principle: always be ready to stop. Especially if we have any kind of longing to be used in ministering healing to the lost, we must be prepared to alter our plans if the need arises. If we are too controlled by our agenda and our priorities, we will find this hard. If, however, our desire is to be like Jesus, who only did what he saw the Father doing, then we will be prepared to stop when God tells us to.

About eighteen months ago I had just had lunch after a busy Monday morning staff meeting. I had three hours in which to write a talk that I was due to deliver to church leaders in London the following morning. Before starting my preparation, I decided to go very quickly to the bank in my local community to draw out some money. I dashed into Chorleywood and used the cash machine.

As I turned round to hurry back to my home, I saw two people walking towards me. One of them I recognized as the husband of a lady that my wife had befriended at the local school. This lady was very much into the New Age and not really interested in coming to our church. She had come a few times five years ago but had then drifted away. We had continued to pray for her but we had not seen any signs of her coming back.

That day, when I saw her husband, I saw a lady walking with him who was clearly in great distress. She looked incredibly sick and very scared. As I looked more closely I saw that it was indeed the man's wife, but something devastating had happened to her. As I walked towards them I stopped and said hello. I then asked her what the matter was and she told me that she had cancer, that she had had drastic surgery and a number of courses of chemotherapy, and that now the only hope was one more course of radiation treatment a few weeks later. She was in a state of panic, walking the streets in a daze, with her husband who was also traumatized.

At that moment my heart just broke for them and all fear of witnessing frankly went out of the window. I asked them if they would mind me praying for healing. She grabbed hold of my hands and begged me to pray. So there and then, outside the supermarket in our local community, I invited the Holy Spirit to come and asked Jesus to heal the cancer. I finished and the lady seemed peaceful. I then spoke to the husband and gave him my mobile telephone number, telling him that if ever he or his wife needed me to pray more, and talk some more about Jesus, I was available. They only had to call. We parted as a lady from one of our church plants walked by and took both of them to her house for a cup of tea. I then returned home to start work on my talk.

Just as I began to get focused on my preparation, my phone went. It was the husband. 'You know you said that we were to ring if we could have some more prayer?' I said, 'Yes.' 'Well, how about now?' I stopped my preparation and asked them to come to the chapel in our church and there I prayed some more for them, and talked to them about the Lord Jesus. At the end I asked them if they would like an older couple from our church, who have a lot of experience in praying for the sick, to come and visit them in their own home, to continue praying. They said they would, and we set that up.

A few months later my wife Alie was at the school gate picking up one of our four children. As she was standing there, the lady walked up to her and said, 'Please tell Mark, thank you. I have just this morning been to the consultant and he says it's remarkable: I am completely free of the cancer. He's given me the "all clear".' That was a year ago as I write, and I have just seen the lady again attending one of our evangelistic services, looking in perfect health.

Now I tell this story not to make you think that I am some hot-shot healing evangelist but rather to show that what I am sharing is not just an idea in the head but a matter of the heart, and a lifestyle issue as well. If you and I want to be effective in ministering healing to the lost, then – like Jesus – we must always be ready to stop. This may mean a good deal of inconvenience. It may mean that our plans are trashed. But if it means that a sick person is healed and subsequently comes to Jesus, doesn't that make it worthwhile? We need to trust that when this sort of divine interruption occurs, our Father will make up what we have lost. It is interesting to note that the next day that incident gave me a great testimony from which to launch into a rallying cry to the leaders to rediscover the Father's heart for lost people. I most likely would have spent several hours trying to find a good illustration for my talk that day, but the Father knew better. He gave me a testimony that was as relevant and as fresh as it could have been. That taught me something about God's sovereignty.

4. *Always be ready to pray*

I love the conclusion to the story of the healing of blind Bartimaeus:

> *'What do you want me to do for you?' Jesus asked.*
>   *'Teacher,' the blind man said, 'I want to see!'*
>   *And Jesus said to him, 'Go your way. Your faith has healed you.'*
> *And instantly the blind man could see! Then he followed Jesus down the road.*

Jesus simply asks the man what he wants him to do for him. As we saw in Chapter 4, when we looked at models of healing ministry, this is a good example of what is advocated in the Person-Centred model. Jesus does not give any kind of supernatural diagnosis here. He simply asks the man what he wants to receive. The man, not surprisingly, says, 'I want to see.' Far from being passive in the whole encounter, blind Bartimaeus is called into an active role in the healing that happens here. He is asked to confess his need, and in doing so, he admits to having faith in Jesus' God-given ability to heal his blindness. To all this Jesus responds with the briefest possible statement, 'Go your way. Your faith has healed you.'

One thing I have learnt in ministering healing to the lost is the importance of the following principle: **always be ready to pray**. When we are with a lost person who is sick, it is not enough just to sympathize with their need. We must be ready to offer prayer there and then. This should be kept as simple as possible. Whichever model you use, whether it is the Kingdom model of John Wimber (my preference), or the Atonement model of people like Roger Sapp, the key is simplicity and brevity.

In my book *Prophetic Evangelism* (also published by Authentic) I provide a simple list of steps to take.

First, it is really important to be clear about the person's name and their need. You want to mention their names before the Father and you want to be open about their condition. A few minutes in conversation will be enough to get all the vital information.

Second, it is vital to share a very brief testimony with them. Say something like this: 'I am a Christian and I really believe that Jesus saves, Jesus heals, Jesus delivers. We have seen people healed through prayer in Jesus' name.'

Third, always ask the person for permission to pray. Say something like, 'Would you like me to pray for you?'

Fourth, if they say yes, tell them what is involved. Say that it won't take long and that you are going to invite the Holy Spirit to come and minister healing to the condition in Jesus' name. Ask them to extend their arms and hold their hands out to receive.

Fifth, *pray*! There is one golden rule here though: be brief. Jesus did not pray at great length when he ministered healing to those who were not his followers. He prayed simply and with authority. We need to do the same. Religious and lengthy prayers are not necessary and indeed frequently off-putting. Pray succinctly and with faith.

Sixth, track what the Holy Spirit is saying and doing. It is so fascinating the way those who have never heard about what happens when people receive prayer experience the very phenomena we see in church. They experience sensations of warmth, heat, tingling and so on. Their hands may shake and their eyelids flutter. This is the moment to share prophetic words the Lord gives you. Let them bask in the embrace of the Father's love for a few moments after praying.

Seventh, ask them how they feel and what they sensed was going on. Encourage them to believe that God was doing something in their lives. Don't make promises but do point to the things that indicate that God has touched them.

Finally, always point away from yourself when they ask, 'What was that?' Unbelievers will never have experienced anything like this before. It is important that you tell them that it isn't you and it isn't some New Age force field, but the Lord Jesus, who loves them personally. Ask them if they'd like to know more. Direct them to a church where they will receive more of what they have just heard about and experienced.

Ministering healing to the lost

The ministry of divine healing is accordingly one of the greatest and, I suspect, under-used resources that the church has in evangelism today. If we are only concerned about ministering healing to those who go to church we will have missed a great opportunity. To be sure, the congregation is the place to begin this ministry, but it is not the place to end. As with the gift of prophecy, the gifts of healing and miracles are dynamic and potent outside the church, not just inside. Indeed, as I have written in

Prophetic Evangelism, they are often more dynamic and potent among not-yet-Christians than they are with those who are already 'part of the family', as it were. One main reason why I believe this is true has to do with the honour of God's name. This is much more at stake with not-yet-Christians than with Christians. When I'm praying for those who don't know Christ, I am always thinking, 'God, you've got to deliver here. Your name is at stake. If you don't answer, then your name will be discredited. If you do, your name will be truly magnified.' I happen to believe that the Father loves this kind of appeal to his name's sake.

So, to summarize: take the ministry of divine healing out into the streets and the workplace. Learn from Jesus Christ and, on a daily basis:

> Always be ready to act
> Always be ready to listen
> Always be ready to stop
> Always be ready to pray.

Conclusion

For the Glory of God

MARC A. DUPONT

We all experience different levels of love and commitment. In our hearts we each have differing priorities of love and commitment for the different relationships in our lives. In the Greek language there are several words for love, such as *agape*, *phileo* and *eros*. Each of these words has a specific meaning, although they all have to do with love. In the English language we have a problem in that we use the same word for multiple applications. A few years ago in Southern California I saw a car with two bumper stickers. One read, 'I love Jesus' while the other read, 'I love my dog.' While I'm sure the driver could have qualified these two loves if asked, the stickers raised the question of whether his love for God was the same as his love for his dog. In order to step into a healing ministry we need to perceive love from a biblical perspective.

As we have explored in the first chapter of this book, God is a God who heals because of his very nature. He is a God of great glory, not only because of what he has done, but simply because of who he is. When he revealed his glory to Moses on the mountain, he stated:

The LORD, the LORD God, compassionate and gracious, slow to anger, and abounding in loving kindness and truth (Ex. 34:6).

His glory is who he is. His glory is the essential core of himself. God heals because he is a God of amazing compassion. However, if we truly want to establish a vital healing ministry, I believe we must come to grips with the fullness of why God is in the healing business. In other words, we must correctly perceive and understand God's priorities of love. If we don't have such a heart knowledge of God's ways it is easy to get confused as to his priorities. We see such confusion in many churches that put a higher priority on keeping all their meetings very orderly. Such a church might never have a ministry time of praying for hurting people during the service, out of fear that it could get messy or unseemly. In defence of such a posture the leaders might quote 1 Corinthians 14:33, which states, 'God is not a God of confusion but of peace.' While it is true that God is a God of peace, he puts a higher priority on bringing people into healing and abundant life than he does on maintaining dignified church services. Just think of the public spectacle the Father put his only begotten Son through in order to redeem us. As Jesus said, people were not created for the Sabbath, but rather the Sabbath was created for us. God is always more concerned about the reality of love than anything else. The question is, then, what are God's priorities of love?

The three levels of love

At the risk of trying to oversimplify a multifaceted and vast topic, I believe there are three basic levels of Christian love which every believer is called to experience. First is what Jesus referred to as our 'first love' for the person of God. This is almost always what we experience when we first realize that God, Christ, the Cross, our sin, heaven and hell are all true. At the point when we surrender our lives to

Christ as our Lord and Saviour, we have an initial gratitude and deep love for Christ, for his act of sacrifice in saving us. This 'first love' is to be maintained and deepened as we go on with Christ and grow in knowledge of him. Too often, however, like the saints in the church of Ephesus, we can focus so much on the work and things of God that we neglect the person of God. The church of Ephesus was to be commended for many reasons. Jesus said to them:

> *I know your deeds and your toil and perseverance, and that you cannot tolerate evil men, and you put to the test those who call themselves apostles, and they are not, and you found them to be false; and you have perseverance and have endured for my name's sake, and have not grown weary (Rev. 2:2–3).*

However, he continued with a rebuke:

> *But I have this against you, that you have left your first love (Rev. 2:4).*

After coming to Christ and discovering his wonderful love for us, most of us go on to a second important revelation: that he deeply loves others as well as ourselves. Those who have always demonstrated an altruistic nature may find their caring and serving of others is simply strengthened and expanded. Most of us, however, are awakened to a biblical realization that if we are truly going to emulate Christ we must begin to reach out to our neighbours and the needy as God gives us opportunity. The expression of love for others can range from teaching Sunday school to working to help feed the hungry in our cities. It can be something extravagant such as quitting a good career and going on the mission field, or simply cooking a meal for a neighbour who's down with a bad back. A love for others, if truly expressed, always takes the form of action. The Apostle John stated:

Little children, let us not love with word or with tongue, but in deed and truth (1 Jn. 3:18).

God's love and compassion for those who are suffering should propel the body of Christ to pursue God's gifts of healing and establish healing ministries.

There is, however, a third level of love that God calls us to as we mature in our relationship with him, and that is a deep, unquenchable passion for the person of God. While this third level of love may be simply the fulfilment of our first love, it achieves a maturity and depth beyond the former. It means being broken by a desire for more of God simply because of who he is, regardless of the blessings he has for us. Like David, the lover of God, we realize that we truly only desire that one thing: to daily behold God's beauty (Ps. 27:4). This type of love results in a desire to give one's life away in order to see God glorified on earth as he is in the heavens. One ends up yearning to see the fulfilment of Habakkuk's prophecy that 'the knowledge of God's glory will cover the earth, as the waters cover the seas' (Hab. 2:14). In short, out of love for God we are zealous for Christ Jesus to come into his inheritance. We truly desire to see the nations given to him as his inheritance. Moreover, we desire to see the Bridegroom return for the Bride. As John said in his book of revelation:

The Spirit and the bride say, 'Come.' And let the one who hears say, 'Come' (Rev. 22:17).

Indeed, the earth itself is crying out for the healing return of the Lord Jesus, according to the Apostle Paul. It is when we are at that point of abandonment that we begin to realize the Father's bigger picture in creating humanity and then sending Christ to redeem it. It was not so much simply for our sake, but rather for his precious Son Jesus' sake – to raise us as a beautiful bride for him and to give him an inheritance of the nations.

The cry for the glorious return of Christ differs with those who have a mature passion for him. The heart cry for the return of the Lord in a basic first love, while biblically valid, may stem from selfish motivation. To some degree this type of self-centred thinking was prevalent in the Jesus Movement of the late 1960s and early 1970s in California. There was a wholesale focus on the Antichrist and the havoc he would wreak in the 'end times'. This view of the end times was lopsided in that there was no vision of a global move of the Spirit of God that would bring millions, if not billions, into the Kingdom. The numbers of people who have come to Christ since 1974 is staggering. And that statement would still be true if we only counted those that have come to Christ in Asia, South America and Africa. Many cities in the former Soviet Union that had not had the Gospel preached since the Bolshevik Revolution some seventy years earlier have had incredible numbers coming to Christ, and many churches brought into being. I have seen first-hand in some Muslim areas of west Africa thousands come to Christ in communities where the Gospel had not been preached in decades.

An authentic heart cry of 'Come, Lord Jesus' is a rich combination of a hunger to gaze on the actual person of Christ and a hunger to see Christ come into all that the Father has promised him. David, who was a prophet, overheard in the Spirit a conversation that had taken place long before the world was even formed. His song, which today we call Psalm 2, says:

> *I will surely tell of the decree of the LORD: He said to me, 'You are my son, today I have begotten you. Ask of me, and I will surely give the nations as your inheritance and the very ends of the earth as*

your possession. You shall break them with a rod of iron. You shall shatter them like earthenware' (Ps. 2:7–9).

The Apostle Paul prophetically stated that the time will come when 'every knee will bow (before Christ), and every tongue will confess (to his Lordship)'. Our heart cry for the person of Christ should be powerfully permeated with this prophetic desire to see the knowledge of Christ Jesus sweep across our nations, cities and cultures. That is not to say that all will be saved. The Bible clearly says that will not be the case. However, just as the person and works of Christ were fully known throughout all of Israel prior to the passion, so the works and glory of Christ will be known throughout the earth before his return. And just as two thousand years ago that knowledge prompted some to hatred and violence, so it shall again. Indeed, today the number of people being martyred for the Gospel is staggering. According to Todd Nettleton, spokesman of The Voice of the Martyrs, some 160,000 Christians are martyred each year worldwide (WorldNetDaily.com, 20 October 2005). The call going out from the throne of God to the church today is to rise up and behold that the harvest fields are ripe. We are at an unprecedented time in world history of seeing the Good News go forward.

To seek after the Lord for the gifts of healing and miracles is a good thing. It is very much God's heart for each of us to experience the joy of seeing hurting and diseased people set free of their afflictions by Jesus' authority and power. There is a prophetic call from the Holy Spirit beyond that, however, and that is to take up the gifts of the Spirit, much as a soldier entering into battle would pick up his pistol and rifle. As any soldier can testify, it is one thing to win a battle, but another thing altogether to win a war. As soldiers for Christ we are called to win our cities, cultures and even nations for Christ.

On those occasions when I have been in meetings where we have experienced a great many people being healed, there has almost always been a profound sense of the awesomeness of the Lord. Acts 2:43 tells us that: 'everyone [in the early church of Jerusalem] kept feeling a sense of awe; and many wonders and signs were taking place'. I believe that this sense of awe and reverence concerning the person of Christ Jesus is going to be restored to the body of Christ internationally before his return. The bride of Christ, the church, is going to be caught up in a radical and passionate love for her Lord and bridegroom. Just as healings and miracles, signs and wonders were at the heart of the early church, so shall they be again.

We are in the process of catching an incredible wave of God's power that is being released to the church. As any surfer can tell you, however, it's not enough just to see an incoming wave. In order to catch it and then ride it, the surfer must first be paddling. Out of intimacy with God we can seek after his gifts, anointing and opportunities that the church today can catch Holy Spirit momentum. It is by sharing his love for hurting people and, especially, growing in our love for Christ that we can learn to ride the waves he wants to release. Many of us are captive to a fear that God really doesn't want to use 'me' for something so wonderful. God's response is 'Come on in, the water's fine.' Jesus addressed this very fear when he said:

> *If you then, being evil, know how to give good gifts to your children, how much more will your heavenly Father give the Holy Spirit to those who ask him? (Lk. 11:13).*

We are truly living in the last days as Jesus described them. We are in a time of wars and rumours of wars, earthquakes, famines and droughts. We are seeing the love of many grown cold through the deceits of sin, selfishness and hard hearts. In the midst of all of the earthquakes, famines, mud slides, tsunamis, hurricanes and bloodshed this great Gospel of the Kingdom of God is being preached to the nations with great anointing. The words of Mordecai to Esther are prophetically echoing far and wide to the church today: it is 'for such a time as this' that God has placed us on the face of the earth. His Spirit is within us and upon us to set the captives free, to heal the broken hearts, to see the lame walk, the blind see and the deaf hear. The Holy Spirit is anointing the church to run this race that is before us and to give the nations to Christ as his inheritance.

Do not be afraid, little flock, for your Father has chosen gladly to give you the kingdom (Lk. 12:32).

Appendix

School of Ministry Training Course
St Andrew's Church Chorleywood

MARK STIBBE

YOU ARE FREE TO PHOTOCOPY THESE NOTES AND USE THEM
FOR TRAINING PRAYER MINISTRY TEAM MEMBERS IN THE
LOCAL CHURCH.

Aim: *to equip believers to minister to others in the power of the
Spirit, doing the works of Jesus (saving sinners, healing the sick
and delivering the oppressed).*

COURSE OUTLINE

- Our acceptance in the Father
- Operating in the Spirit's power
- Qualities for team members
- Prayer ministry and the spiritual gifts
- Leading a seeker to Christ
- Ministering healing in Jesus' name
- How to deliver the oppressed
- How to hear the voice of God
- The confession of sin
- The practice of prayer ministry
- Extra notes: The laying-on of hands

Session 1

Our Acceptance in the Father

Introduction

Those who serve on a ministry team need to do so from the right motivation. If we are praying for people in order to gain approval, we will not be a help but a hindrance.

What does it mean to serve God with hearts made whole? It means to be like Jesus. Jesus lived in 'The Cycle of Grace'. He knew he was accepted by Abba. Ministry flowed out of intimacy.

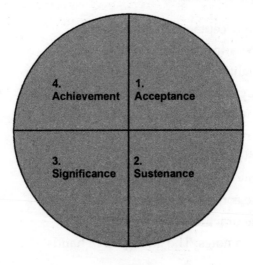

In his book *Clinical Theology*, Frank Lake writes that this cycle is the key to Jesus' ministry. It represents the spirit of *life* in Jesus Christ. It is the secret of his well-being.

Lake argues that living in this cycle is the secret to our well-being as well. As healed people, we will be conduits of God's wholeness to others. The key to ministry is therefore to be like *Jesus*.

ACCEPTANCE. Jesus heard the Father saying, 'You are my Son, whom I love; with you I am well pleased.' Jesus gained his sense of acceptance from his position, not his performance.

SUSTENANCE. This knowledge of Abba's gracious acceptance sustained Jesus throughout his ministry. How was it sustained? By the Word and by the Spirit.

a) The Word
b) The Spirit

SIGNIFICANCE. This in turn invested Jesus with a sense of his self-worth. It enabled him to be *free to be*. Thus Jesus can be perfectly open about his identity (see the 'I am' sayings, NIV).

I am the _____ of life (Jn. 6:48)

I am the _____ of the world (Jn. 8:12)

I am the _____ (Jn. 10:9)

I am the _____ (Jn. 10:14)

I am the _____ (Jn. 11:25)

I am the _____ (Jn. 14:6)

I am the _____ (Jn. 15:1)

Session 1

ACHIEVEMENT. On the Cross, Jesus cried, 'It is finished!' This is the exclamation of a winner – of one who seized his God-given destiny and succeeded in doing the work God gave him.

When we look at our own lives, what is the foundation for our ministry? Do we know Abba's acceptance, affirmation and approval? Or do we have a drive to earn them?

LOOKING AT OURSELVES

ACCEPTANCE. We receive a sense of the Father's acceptance through the 'Spirit of adoption'. (Rom. 8:15–16; Gal. 4:4–6). To live in the fullness of this, we need to deal with:

- Wrong theology
- Rejection
- Unforgiveness
- Lies and curses
- Other

SUSTENANCE. The Spirit and the Word testify that we are the adopted children of God. Ministry team members need to stand on God's promises and go on soaking in the Spirit.

a) The Word
b) The Spirit

SIGNIFICANCE. It is this revelation of the Father's love that sets us free to be who we really are. Ministry team members need to know this significance in the Word and the Spirit:

I have been given authority to be a child of God (Jn. 1:12)

I was predestined for adoption (Eph. 1:5)

I am a child of Abba by adoption (Rom. 8:15)

I am God's work of art (Eph. 2:10)

I am no longer under any condemnation (Rom. 8:1)

I cannot be separated from the Father's love (Rom. 8:35)

I am no longer a slave but a son (Gal. 4:7)

I am seated with the Son in heaven (Eph. 2:6)

ACHIEVEMENT. This revelation enables us to minister without striving. We are no longer driven by whips but drawn by cords of love. We walk in the love of God and give it away.

Remember, ministry flows out of intimacy!

Conclusion

What's the lesson? Don't turn the cycle of grace into a cycle of law. Renounce any performance mentality. Help others to experience the glorious freedom of the children of God.

Some great quotes

Bring me a church made up of God's children, a company of men and women whose faces shine with their Heavenly Father's smile, who are accustomed to take their cares and cast them on their Father as children should, who know they are accepted and beloved, and are perfectly content with their great Father's will; put them down in the middle of a group of ungodly people, and I will guarantee that they will begin to be jealous of their peace and joy. In this way happy saints become the most effective workers on the minds of the unsaved.

Charles Spurgeon

When the love of God impacts your heart to the fullest, no mountain is too tall, no ocean too broad, no valley too deep that you would not go through it for him. That kind of love will cause you to serve like nothing else can. Then, rather than working for him, you are working with him to reach the nations of this world.

John Arnott

For further reading

Mark Stibbe, *From Orphans to Heirs. Celebrating Our Spiritual Adoption* (Bible Reading Fellowship).

Session 2

Operating in the Spirit's Power

Introduction

Jesus said the harvest is plentiful but the workers are few (Mt. 9:35–38). Jesus wants *Kingdom workers*. To put it another way, he wants us to be

BA: Born Again by the power of the Spirit
MA: Marvellously Altered by the power of the Spirit
PhD: Preaching, Healing, Delivering in the power of the Spirit

Ministry team members are people anointed and trained to share the Good News, heal the sick and deliver the oppressed. They are not just believers, nor just disciples, but Kingdom workers too.

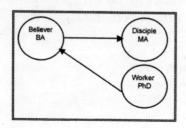

The worker is someone who has come to faith in Jesus Christ (BA), who is growing in wholeness and holiness (MA) and who is equipped to be an agent of the Kingdom (PhD).

An effective worker understands that the reign of God only advances through the Spirit's power. This is because the Holy Spirit *is* the power of the Kingdom.

Ministry team members are Kingdom people!

1. Kingdom vision The Kingdom of God is the dynamic rule of God invading enemy territory. We live in the 'now' and the 'not yet' of the Kingdom.

- the *now* of the Kingdom, Matthew 12:28 (D Day)
- the *not yet* of the Kingdom, Matthew 6:10 (VE Day)

2. Kingdom advance. There are two main ways in which the Kingdom of God advances: through words and works. For these we need authority and power (Lk. 9:1–2).

- authority, the right to do something (*exousia*)
- power, the might to do something (*dunamis*)

3. Kingdom resources. We cannot preach the message or perform miracles in our own strength (Acts 3:12). The Holy Spirit gives us supernatural gifts to do the Kingdom's work:

word of knowledge
word of wisdom
faith
healing gifts

miraculous works
prophecy
discernment
tongues
interpretation

4. Kingdom workers. The Lord chooses the foolish to confound the wise. So he uses ordinary subjects to do extraordinary exploits (Mt. 10:2–4; Acts 4:13; 1 Cor. 1:26–29).

GOD CALLED YOU ... If you ever feel unworthy, you're in good company:

Moses stuttered.

David's armour didn't fit.

John Mark was rejected by Paul.

Timothy had ulcers.

Hosea's wife was a prostitute.

Amos' only training was in the school of fig tree pruning.

Jacob was a liar.

David had an affair.

Solomon was too rich.

Jesus was too poor.

Abraham was too old.

David was too young.

Peter was afraid of death.

Lazarus was dead.

John was self-righteous.

Naomi was a widow.

Paul was a murderer.

So was Moses.

Jonah ran from God.

Miriam was a gossip.

Gideon and Thomas both doubted.

Jeremiah was a depressive.

Elijah was burned out.

John the Baptist was a loudmouth.

Martha was a worrier.

Her sister may have been lazy.

Samson had long hair.

Noah got drunk.

Did I mention that Moses had a short fuse?

So did Peter, Paul – well, lots of folks did.

But God doesn't require a job interview. He doesn't hire and fire like most bosses, because he's more our Dad than our boss. He doesn't look at financial gain or loss. He's not prejudiced or partial, not judging, grudging, not deaf to our cry, not blind to our need. No matter how much we try, God's gifts are free.

Conclusion

Ministry team members need to operate in the Spirit's power. This means being constantly filled with the Spirit (Zech. 4:6; Eph. 5:18).

The testimony of countless men and women over the centuries is this: that they only became effective workers for the harvest once they had been filled with the Spirit. Note the following UK giants:

Being in secret prayer I felt suddenly my heart melting within me like wax before a fire, with love to God my Saviour. I felt not only love and peace, but also a longing to be dissolved and to be with Christ; and there was a cry in my inmost soul, with which I was totally unacquainted before, it was this – 'Abba, Father; Abba, Father.' I could not help calling God my Father: I knew that I was his child, and that he loved me; my soul being filled and satiated, crying, 'It is enough – I am satisfied; give me strength and I will follow thee through fire and water.' I could now say that I was happy indeed. There was in me 'a well of water, springing up into everlasting life', yea, the love of God was shed abroad in my heart by the Holy Ghost.

Howel Harris (June 1735)

The Spirit itself bore witness to my spirit that I was a child of God, gave me an *evidence* hereof, and I immediately cried, 'Abba, Father!' And this I did ... before I reflected on, or was conscious of, any fruit of the Spirit. It was from this testimony that love, joy, peace, and the whole fruit of the Spirit flowed.

John Wesley (May 1738)

For further reading

David Pytches, *Come, Holy Spirit* (Hodder & Stoughton).

Session 3

Qualities for Team Members

Introduction

To be on a ministry team in the local church, something more than just charisma (i.e. anointing) is required. Character is vital as well.

You may flow in all nine gifts of the Spirit listed in 1 Corinthians 12:8–11 (though it's unlikely!), but if you lack the nine flavours of the Spirit's fruit (Gal. 5:22–23) your suitability will be questioned:

Love Joy Peace	relationship with God
Patience Kindness Goodness	relationship with others
Faithfulness Gentleness Self-control	relationship with self

This means that *character is as important as charisma in prayer ministry.* What are the chief qualities needed for a ministry team member in the local church?

1. **Maturity.** The mature Christian knows his or her position in Christ and is assured of the Father's affection and affirmation. There is therefore no striving or performance-orientation.

The mature believer loves God passionately and loves their neighbour *as themselves*. This is walking in the love of God and giving it away.

Passion for God is shed abroad in the heart of such a person. There is an ability to receive as well as give (so as to minister out of the overflow). NB You can't give what you don't have.

2. **Accountability.** Another vital quality (Heb. 13:17). We are not looking for lone rangers with an independent spirit (Rom. 12:4f). Nor are we looking for Flash Gordons with a Messiah complex ('Fourteen and a half minutes to save the world!').

We are looking for people who are full members of their local church – people who submit to authority, who are part of a small group, and who give their time, talents and treasure.

Accountability means that you accept the judgment of your leaders and peers about your suitability for this ministry and your place in it, and you are also able to take correction (Prov. 15:32).

3. **Purity.** Needless to say, ministry team members need to be making personal purity a priority in their lives. This is particularly important in the area of relationships.

If we allow ourselves to become angry with another member of the body of Christ, this will grieve the Spirit and stop the flow. Forgiveness releases the fire of God (Mk. 11:25).

Members need to be peacemakers, avoiding factional comments and working to maintain the unity of the Spirit. This means denominational neutrality (1 Cor. 3:1–11).

4. Humility. It is imperative not to become proud, especially if God starts to use us powerfully. We need to keep low and not think of ourselves more highly than we ought (Rom. 12:3).

Cultivating and maintaining a servant heart is essential (Phil. 2:5–11; Mk. 10:45). Jesus humbled himself and became a slave, even washing his disciples' feet.

God 'gives grace to the humble' (Jas. 4:6, NIV). The lower we become, the higher we'll go. The weaker we feel, the more powerful our prayers will be (2 Cor. 12:9).

5. Flexibility. While we want every ministry team member to work within the guidelines, we also want to be open to the Spirit's prompting at all times. Flexibility within a framework is key.

See Philip's example in Acts 8. At the start of the chapter he is ministering in a city to crowds. At the end he is ministering in the desert to an individual. He is the model of flexibility.

The crucial thing is not to be inflexible. Some people tend to see things every time in one particular way (e.g. everything is due to demons). We need to be like soft clay in the Potter's hands.

6. Consistency. Ministry team members need to be consistent and faithful people. They need to be people who don't grow weary in doing good (Gal. 6:9).

They need to be consistent in prayer (especially for the leader of the service, preacher, worship leader, singers/musicians, congregation, other team members, for the needy, etc.).

They need to be consistent in their study of the Word of God, because it is the Word of God that penetrates between soul and spirit (Heb. 4:12). You can only speak out what you know.

7. Compassion. The crowning quality. You can have all the spiritual gifts that are going, but if you lack love for the lost and the hurting, it all counts for nothing.

Seven is the perfect number. Compassion is the most important quality of all. Jesus 'had compassion on them' (Mt. 9:36, NIV). The word signifies a deep, gut-level sympathy.

Why did Jesus feel so deeply? It says in verse 36, 'because they were harassed and helpless'. Compassion is the opposite of condemnation (Mt. 7:1ff; Jn. 4:17–18).

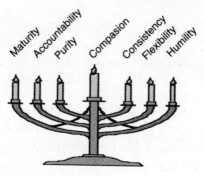

Conclusion

Character is as important as charisma. Jesus warns that personal obedience qualifies us for heaven, *not* the gift of prophecy or a ministry of miracles.

> *Not everyone who says to me, 'Lord, Lord,' will enter the kingdom of heaven, but only he who does the will of my Father who is in heaven. Many will say to me on that day, 'Lord, Lord, did we not prophesy in your name, and in your name drive out demons and perform many miracles?' Then I will tell them plainly, 'I never knew you. Away from me, you evildoers!' (Mt. 7:21–23, NIV).*

Session 4

Prayer Ministry
and the Spiritual Gifts

Introduction

We believe in getting the right people into the right ministries for the right reasons. To do that, everyone needs to know their God-given S–H–A–P–E (Rick Warren).

Spiritual gifts

Heart

Abilities

Personality

Experience

1. S – Spiritual gifts

What are your spiritual gifts? Every believer has at least one gift and others that cluster around it. One of the classic lists of the spiritual gifts is in 1 Corinthians 12:8–11:

a. Gifts of communication: knowledge and wisdom

Knowledge = the God-given ability to receive and communicate a spiritual insight.

Wisdom = the God-given ability to receive and communicate a message that brings clarity to a complex situation or subject.

b. *Gifts of power: faith, healing, miracles*

Faith = the God-given confidence that the Holy Spirit is about to bring about an extraordinary breakthrough.

Healing = the God-given ability to heal those who are physically, emotionally or spiritually sick.

Miracles = the God-given ability to perform signs and wonders (e.g. resurrection miracles, nature miracles, dramatic healing, etc.).

c. *Gifts of revelation: discernment and prophecy*

Discernment = the God-given ability to discern whether something is due to the Holy Spirit, the human spirit or an unholy spirit.

Prophecy = the God-given ability to receive specific, supernatural revelation for a person or a situation.

d. *Gifts of adoration: tongues and interpretation*

Tongues = ordinarily, the God-given ability to speak out words of praise to the Father in the language of the Spirit.

Interpretation = the special, God-given ability to interpret into English a tongue that has been uttered publicly.

Which of the above gifts are vital for prayer ministry? Do your particular spiritual gifts suggest that you are suited to prayer ministry? How do you score on the S of the word SHAPE?

2. H – Heart

What are you passionate about? Are you passionate about prayer ministry? Is it your desire to see the lost saved, the wounded healed and the oppressed set free?

When Jesus saw the harassed and helpless crowds, he had *compassion* on them (Mt. 9:35–38). A ministry team member needs to know the Father's heart for those who suffer.

Do you have a heart for prayer ministry? If you do not, you will find the commitment overwhelming, the task draining, the motivation impossible and the prospect unwelcome.

3. A – Abilities

Obviously we are not talking about a natural, human ability. We are talking about the anointing of the Holy Spirit for a particular task.

Remember that the gifts of the Spirit are *grace* gifts, not natural talents or human trophies. Do you have the supernatural ability or anointing for this ministry? Have you been effective?

Once we know we are *able* to pray effectively for salvation, healing and deliverance, we can then move on from exercising the gift to exercising the ministry.

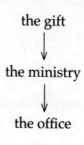

the gift

↓

the ministry

↓

the office

4. P – Personality

John Wimber used to say that the personality he was looking for in the prayer ministry could be summed up by the word FATSO:

Faithful

Available

Teachable

Spirit-filled

Outward-going

The chief quality of course is love (1 Cor. 13). In the last session (Session 3) we looked in depth at the qualities required for prayer ministry. Do you have the right personality for the task?

5. E – Experience

Are you born again and being marvellously altered? Do any of your past experiences lead you to believe that you are called to prayer ministry?

Are you the right S–H–A–P–E for this ministry? Are you going to be the right *person in the* right *ministry for the* right *reason?*

Conclusion

We cannot do this ministry without the gifts of the Spirit. Of particular importance are the gifts of power (faith, healing gifts, miracles) and revelation (discernment and prophecy).

We need to grow in these if we are to be effective workers for the harvest. Jesus operated in the power and the gifts of the Holy Spirit during his ministry. Why should we be any different?

For further reading

Mark Stibbe, *Know Your Spiritual Gifts* (Marshall Pickering).

Session 5

Leading a Seeker to Christ

Introduction

PhD: the P stands for proclamation of the Good News. The ministry team member is one who is trained to witness to a seeker and to lead that person to faith in Jesus.

In this session we focus on a simple way of ministering to seekers. This is based on the same structure as John Wimber's five-step model for healing prayer (see Session 6).

INTERVIEW. Getting to know the person. 'What is your name?' 'What is your need?' Be friendly! But also be discerning: the person may come for healing when they really need salvation.

DIAGNOSIS. Where is this person in relation to God? The following is taken from the parable of the Prodigal Son. Where would you put the person in relation to these five stages? (With thanks to Steve Croft.)

1. **RUNNING FAR AWAY FROM FATHER GOD**
   (Lk. 15:11–12)

2. **LIVING A SELF-DESTRUCTIVE LIFESTYLE**
   (Lk. 15:13–16)

3. **WAKING UP AND TURNING FROM SIN**
   (Lk. 15:18–19)

4. **RUNNING HOME TO THE FATHER'S ARMS**
   (Lk. 15:20–21)

5. REJOICING IN THE LORD'S ACCEPTANCE
   (Lk. 15:22–24)

So, as you diagnose the situation, is the person under conviction of sin? Is there evidence of godly sorrow and the need for forgiveness? Do they want to be saved?

PRAYER SELECTION. This depends on where this person is with God. Are they ready to receive Christ? You have to discern. Are you *sowing* or are you *reaping*?

If sowing, pray for the Lord to meet their needs. We want the person to experience the Father's love. If reaping, talk the person through the sinner's prayer:

> *Lord Jesus, thank you that you love me. I need you.*
> *Thank you that you died on the Cross for me.*
> *Forgive my disobedience and my sin.*
> *Today I receive you into my life as Saviour and King.*
> *Fill me with your Holy Spirit and change me.*
> *I give you all my life now, that you may lead and guide it.*
> *Thank you Lord for hearing my prayer.*

Then pronounce forgiveness over their lives (Jn. 20:23).

PRAYER. It is important to allow people space to express godly sorrow in repentance and not to intrude too quickly.

When they have finished praying, you need to wait on the Lord. Further ministry may be needed here. Ask the Holy Spirit if there are any issues he wants to deal with now.

POST-PRAYER DIRECTION. If they have just accepted Christ, tell them about your Alpha and Beta courses. There must be follow-up. There are too many decisions, not enough disciples. Use a card like this:

NAME ....

ADDRESS ....

....

....

TEL NO. ....

NAME OF MINISTRY TEAM MEMBER

....

INVITATION TO ALPHA GIVEN? YES / NO

Conclusion

Complete conversion-initiation takes time. What is involved? *Repentance, faith, water baptism, baptism in the Spirit.* Don't be in a hurry unless God says so.

For further reading
J. John, *Calling Out* (Authentic).

Session 6

Ministering Healing in Jesus' Name

Introduction

In the list of the spiritual gifts in 1 Corinthians 12:8–11, Paul mentions 'gifts of healing' (literally, 'gifts of healings', implying variety). What did Paul mean by this? Here is a definition:

> The healing gifts are best understood as the special, charismatic ability to heal illness in the power of the Holy Spirit, and through faith in Jesus Christ. This ability is given to people in the Body of Christ, and they are expected to use this gift faithfully and continuously until the Lord Jesus returns and does away with sickness forever.

There are three basic models for praying for the sick. All three of these are biblical in the sense that they have a foundation in the Scriptures:

- the 'healing evangelist' model
- the 'sacramental ministry' model
- the 'every member' model

John Wimber's ministry taught us the vital principle that everyone can pray for the sick effectively and with authority. We therefore emphasize the 'every member' model.

There is a difference, however, between the gifts, the ministry and the office. The gifts of healing can develop into a ministry of healing, and this ministry can develop into an office.

We believe that Jesus still heals the sick today. At a practical level, we need to pray for the sick and ask God to make them well. How do we do this?

- by imitating Jesus (see John 5:1–15)
- by taking the person through the following five steps

INTERVIEW. In John 5:6–7 Jesus 'learned' that the man had been an invalid for thirty-eight years. He was prepared to ask questions as well as rely on the revelation given by the Holy Spirit.

This shows that there are two levels to the interview: a) Natural ('What is your need?'); b) Supernatural ('What are you doing, Father?' [Jn. 5:19]). We need to listen at both levels.

DIAGNOSIS. Why does Jesus ask, 'Do you want to get well?' (Jn. 5:6, NIV). Is it because he has discerned something in the man's soul? What had happened thirty-eight years prior to this?

We are made up of spirit, soul and body (the soul comprising the mind, emotions and will). Jesus wants to bring healing to the *whole* person. This is what is meant by 'salvation'.

PRAYER SELECTION. This is not just physical healing. This man needed to be set free from his disability. But there was also something in his soul that needed addressing.

So the selection of the prayer was important. Notice Jesus' three commands here. Jesus is seeing whether the man has any faith for his own healing (see also Mk. 3:5; Jn. 9:7).

PRAYER. Here are twelve tips for praying for the sick:

a. Pray in twos or threes (Lk. 10:1). This always allows someone to act as a catcher. It also means that there are more gifts being exercised. It finally guards us against false accusations.

b. Don't pray alone with someone of the opposite sex (2 Tim. 3:6). This should only be allowed when a member of staff has given permission because of numbers.

c. Lay hands gently and appropriately on the afflicted area (Mk. 16:18). There is no need to force anything. Men must not lay their hands on a woman's body, and vice versa.

d. Welcome the Holy Spirit. This ministry is not like the National Health. It is not *us* curing the person through medical means. It is Jesus, through the power of the Spirit (Acts 3:16).

e. Anoint the person with oil. In Mark 6:13 the twelve anointed the sick with oil and they were healed. If there is a leader present, ask them to anoint the sick person with oil (Jas. 5:14).

f. Keep your eyes open! When Peter prayed for the sick man at the Gate Beautiful, it says 'he looked straight at him' (Acts 3:4, NIV). Always remember to *watch and pray*.

g. Be sensitive to signs of the Spirit, i.e. manifestations of God's power (1 Cor. 14:25). We may feel heat, tingling, shaking; the person being prayed for may too – plus falling, laughing, peace, tears, etc.

h. Exercise discernment (compare Mark 9:25–27 with Mark 7:32–35). Be open to further prophetic revelation. Fred Grewe says there are five common ways to receive this:

a picture	(see it)
a headline	(read it)
a sensation	(feel it)
an impression	(think it)
a word	(say it)

i. Speak to the condition with authority. We have authority to pray for healing, and there is power in the name of Jesus. So let's be bold. Especially in the context of the lost (Acts 3:6).

j. Treat the person with love. If you are praying in the Spirit (i.e. in tongues) do so quietly. Don't manipulate, put off or frighten. Give the person time. Allay fears (Lk. 11:13).

k. Ask the person what they sense God is doing. In Mark 8:23, when Jesus was praying for a blind man, he asked him what he saw. He then prayed a second time.

l. Always give thanks to the Lord for what he has done (Lk. 17:18). It is more important to bless the Father for what he is doing than to ask the Father to bless what we are doing.

POST-PRAYER DIRECTION. 'Stop sinning or something worse may happen' (Jn. 5:14, NIV). Jesus warned the man that he could lose his healing. Help people from disease to discipleship (Mk. 10:52).

Conclusion

Do persevere: 'You'll see more people healed when you pray for more people!' We minister on the border between miracle and mystery. Healing flows from the Cross. But it can be:

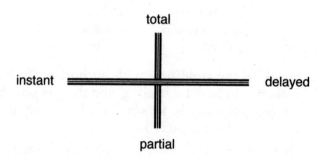

total

instant   delayed

partial

For further reading
John Woolmer, *Healing and Deliverance* (Monarch).

Session 7

How to Deliver the Oppressed

Introduction

Jesus gave us power and authority to preach, heal and deliver. So how do we do deliverance? How do we set people free from evil spirits?

Again we use a five-step model. Before using this model, however, it is imperative for the ministry team members to *prepare* properly. No one goes into battle without the right kit:

1. Pray for forgiveness for any sin (Jas. 5:16).
2. Ask the Lord for the power of the Spirit (2 Cor. 10:4).
3. Pray for the gift of discernment (1 Jn. 4:2; 1 Cor. 12:10).
4. Put on the armour of God (Eph. 6:10ff).
5. Stand on God's promises (1 Jn. 3:8, 4:4; Col. 2:15).
6. Remind yourself of your position in Christ (Eph. 2:6).
7. Remember your church's ministry guidelines (Heb. 13:17).

INTERVIEW. Are there signs of the person being demonized?

> Aggression
> Bodily contortions
> Animal noises or actions
> Violent coughing
> Very violent shaking
> Vomiting or retching
> Pressure on the head and the shoulders
> Unholy voice
> Maniacal laughter
> Contorted facial expression
> Intense fear
> Screaming or shrieking
> Blaspheming and/or foul language
> Demonic tongues
> Behaviour suggestive of sexual sin
> Nightmares
> Other

You will obviously not get all of these manifestations of an evil spirit in one person. But be advised: in the presence of the Holy Spirit, unholy spirits surface. There is, in short, a power encounter.

DIAGNOSIS. If the person starts manifesting in one or more of the ways above, you need to get to the root of the problem. Where has this person opened a door to the demonic?

Have you ever been involved in the occult?
Has your family, back to your great-grandparents?
Have you ever been cursed?
Have you ever been involved in a cult or a false religion?

Have you ever been involved in sexual immorality?
Have you any addictions in your life?
Have you ever been an alcoholic?
Have you allowed past hurts to control your life?
Have you a problem with anger or bitterness?
Have you unforgiveness in your life?

Diagnosis involves identifying the entry points. These are described in Galatians 5:19–21. Here Paul lists activities that disqualify people from the Kingdom of God. These can be grouped as:

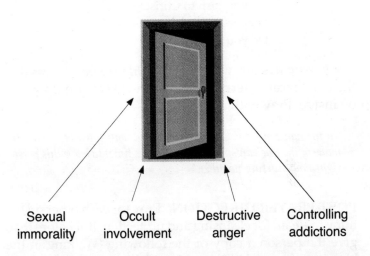

| Sexual immorality | Occult involvement | Destructive anger | Controlling addictions |

PRAYER SELECTION. If the person clearly requires deliverance from an evil spirit (or evil spirits), there are three rules in the way we pray:

   a. Exercise compassion. Hate the demon, not the person. Remember the dignity of the person.

b. Speak in a calm voice. Shouting is unnecessary and creates the feeling that the person is being condemned or told off.

c. Look the person in the eye. If a person is demonized, there is often something in that person's gaze.

PRAYER. What, then, of the prayer ministry? Two or three should pray for the person in an undisturbed place. You need the cooperation of the person. Ask these three baptismal questions:

> Do you turn to Christ?
> Do you repent of your sins?
> Do you renounce evil?

The person has free will. *Do you want to be free?* Stress that the person can interrupt at any time to say what's going on inside. Pray with authority:

> *'In the name of Jesus Christ, I command you, spirit of ... (use the name of the unclean spirits here, one at a time) to leave this person right now, hurting no other.'*

POST-PRAYER DIRECTION. Pray for each other on the ministry team for cleansing and protection. But before that, give the person a copy of the following 'Walking in the blessing of your deliverance' guidelines.

WALKING IN THE BLESSING OF YOUR DELIVERANCE (with thanks to Brownsville Church)

Evil spirits try to return to the vacated house (Mt. 12: 43–44). Satan withdraws but will want to attack again (Lk. 4:13; 2 Pet. 2:20–22). To keep your healing, observe the following:

- Keep walking in the light, cleansed by the blood (1 Jn. 1:6–9)
- Be continuously filled with the Holy Spirit (Eph. 5:18)
- Know and use the Scriptures (Mt. 4:1–11)
- Wear the whole armour of God (Eph. 6:10–18)
- Keep your mind focused on godly things (Phil. 4:8)
- Cultivate a life of praise (2 Chron. 20:21–22)
- Don't be angry or divisive (Eph. 4:26–27)
- Keep yourself sexually pure (1 Thess. 4:3–8)
- Avoid people who are a bad influence (Prov. 2:18–19, 14:7)
- Don't have anything to do with the occult (Deut. 18:9–13)
- Pray every day (Mt. 6:11–13)
- Use the divine power God has given you (2 Cor. 10:3–5)
- Remember your position in Christ (Eph. 2:6)
- Don't allow yourself to become a lover of money (1 Tim. 6:10)
- Keep your home free from all vile things (Ps. 101:2–3)

REMEMBER: 'Resist the devil, and he will flee from you' (Jas. 4:7). In other words, every time the enemy tries to tempt you into opening a door to him, shut it right in his face.

For further reading

Francis MacNutt, *Deliverance from Evil Spirits* (Hodder & Stoughton).

Session 8

How to Hear the Voice of God

Prophecy is the supernatural ability to perceive and to speak out how God sees a person or a situation. Jesus had this spiritual gift and used it to great effect in his ministry. For example

- John 1:40–42 (with Simon)
- John 4:18–19 (with the Samaritan woman)
- Luke 19:1–10 (with Zacchaeus)

Thanks to the outpouring of the Holy Spirit on the Day of Pentecost, every believer can now prophesy. However, even though every believer *can* prophesy, not every believer *does*.

In this session we are going to learn how to hear God's voice. The gift of prophecy is essential for all prayer ministry members since it gets straight to the heart of the matter, the matter of the heart.

We are going to focus on one episode in the life of Jesus to illustrate the *what*, the *how* and the *why* of hearing God's voice. This is in John 1:43–51.

The next day Jesus decided to leave for Galilee. Finding Philip, he said to him, 'Follow me.' Philip, like Andrew and Peter, was from the town of Bethsaida. Philip found Nathanael and told him, 'We have found the one Moses wrote about in the Law, and about whom the prophets also wrote – Jesus of Nazareth, the son of Joseph.' 'Nazareth! Can anything good come from there?' Nathanael asked. 'Come and see,' said Philip (Jn. 1:43–46, NIV).

HEARING THE VOICE OF GOD: THE 'WHAT'

When Jesus looked at Nathanael, he saw three things as a result of revelation. The first had to do with his present, the second had to do with his past, the third with his future.

1. THE PRESENT

John 1:47:

When Jesus saw Nathanael approaching, he said of him, 'Here is a true Israelite, in whom there is nothing false' (NIV).

This is an insight into *character*.

2. THE PAST

John 1:48:

Jesus answered, 'I saw you while you were still under the fig tree before Philip called you' (NIV).

This is an insight into *conduct*.

3. THE FUTURE

John 1:50–51:

> *Jesus said, 'You believe because I told you I saw you under the fig tree. You shall see greater things than that.' He then added, 'I tell you the truth, you shall see heaven open, and the angels of God ascending and descending on the Son of Man' (NIV).*

This is an insight into *calling*.

The observations above show how prophecy should not be restricted to 'foretelling' alone. It is any insight into a person's life or into a situation that reveals God's thoughts.

HEARING THE VOICE OF GOD: THE 'HOW'

Jesus says in John 12:49, 'For I did not speak of my own accord, but the Father who sent me commanded me what to say and how to say it' (NIV). Jesus received the *how* as well as the *what*.

Here are some of the ways we receive prophetic revelation:

A vision/picture	(see it/paint it)
A dream	(interpret it)
An open vision	(engage with it)
A Scripture	(read it)
A sensation	(feel it)
An impression	(think it)
A message	(say it)
A poem	(recite it)
A pun/riddle	(decipher it)

In the story of Nathanael, it seems as if Jesus receives the following:

Impression   An insight about a person (see John 2:25).
Vision   Jesus says, 'I saw you.'
Scripture   Note the language of Genesis 28 here:

He [Jacob] had a dream in which he saw a stairway resting on the earth, with its top reaching to heaven, and the angels of God were ascending and descending on it. There above it stood the LORD, and he said: 'I am the LORD, the God of your father Abraham and the God of Isaac. I will give you and your descendants the land on which you are lying. Your descendants will be like the dust of the earth, and you will spread out to the west and to the east, to the north and to the south. All peoples on earth will be blessed through you and your offspring. I am with you and will watch over you wherever you go, and I will bring you back to this land. I will not leave you until I have done what I have promised you' (Gen. 28: 12–15, NIV).

HEARING THE VOICE OF GOD: THE 'WHY'

Human beings are made up of spirit, soul and body. This can be likened to the Temple in Jerusalem – the spirit is the innermost sanctuary, the soul the holy place, the body the outer court.

A genuine prophetic word exposes hidden things, resulting in a person first of all expressing surprise ('How do you know me?' verse 48), which makes them open to receive the Father's love.

Secondly, genuine prophecy results in faith in Jesus Christ. 'Then Nathanael declared, "Rabbi, you are the Son of God; you are the King of Israel"' (verse 49).

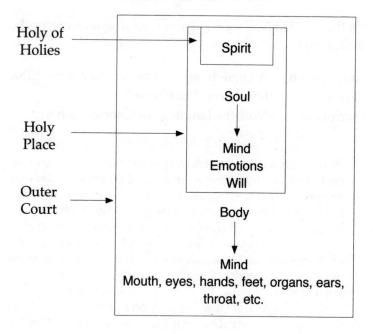

This is the ultimate goal of all prophecy, to open people's eyes to the wonder of who Jesus is (Rev. 19:10). We must learn to hear the voice of God when ministering to others.

Session 9

The Confession of Sin

Introduction

One of the biggest areas of neglect in the church has been to do with repentance. We have all too often assumed that those coming forward for ministry are free from sin.

In the healing presence of God, they come forward to receive help. Just as our shadows become visible as we step into the sunlight, so hurts and sins are revealed in the light of God's love.

THE HUMAN SHADOW

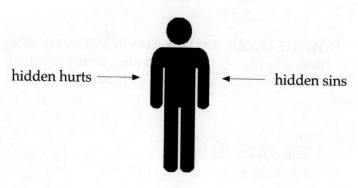

hidden hurts ⟶ ⟵ hidden sins

The spiritual gift of prophecy is essential when we are praying for people. Through prophetic revelation, sins are sometimes exposed as well as wounds. 1 Corinthians 14:24–25 (NIV) says

> *If an unbeliever or someone who does not understand comes in [to a place of worship] while everybody is prophesying, he will be convinced by all that he is a sinner and will be judged by all, and the secrets of his heart will be laid bare. So he will fall down and worship God, exclaiming, 'God is really among you!'*

Paul is clearly saying here that secrets of unbelievers' hearts are disclosed through spoken prophecy. The result is that the sinner falls down, worships, and acknowledges the presence of God.

  a. Application to unbelievers: the woman of Samaria (Jn. 4:4–42).
  b. Application to believers: King David (2 Sam. 12:1–15).

All this highlights how important it is for ministry team members to be trained in the whole area of 'the confession of sin'. What are the vital things to remember here?

1. HOW TO ENCOURAGE A CONFESSION OF SIN:
The motivation for confessing sin lies in the fact that through it we receive a number of blessings from the Lord:

  • mercy (Prov. 28:13)
  • healing (Jas. 5:16)
  • forgiveness and cleansing (1 Jn. 1:9)

2. HOW TO HEAR A CONFESSION OF SIN: It is important to do this right, otherwise the person will not feel sufficiently secure to make a full and honest confession.

- gently (Gal. 6:1)
- compassionately (Mt. 7:1–5)
- thoroughly (Col. 3:5–10)
- discerningly (Jn. 4:17–18)
- confidentially (Prov. 27:6)
- patiently (Ps. 30:5)

3. HOW TO ASSESS A CONFESSION OF SIN: The true nature of repentance involves a change of mind, a change of heart and also a change of behaviour. Do you witness these things?

- change of mind (Ps. 51:3)
- change of heart (Lk. 18:13)
- change of behaviour (Acts 19:17–20)

4. HOW TO RESPOND TO A CONFESSION OF SIN: Remind the person of the Calvary love of God, that 'Jesus came to rub it out, not to rub it in'. Take the person to the Cross for *forgiveness*.

'If you forgive anyone his sins, they are forgiven; if you do not forgive them, they are not forgiven' (Jn. 20:23, NIV). Take seriously your right and responsibility to pronounce forgiveness. We are all priests of the Kingdom of God (1 Pet. 2:9). We can release others from their sins.

Base your assurance on the Word of God, not just your own thoughts. For example, Psalm 103:12 (NIV): 'As far as the east is from the west, so far has he removed our transgressions from us.'

Conclusion

One of the biggest blockages to a person receiving healing and/or deliverance is the hidden presence of anger, bitterness and unforgiveness in their hearts.

There is so much teaching in the New Testament about the need to forgive others (Mt. 6:14–15, 18:21–22, 35; Mk. 11:24–25; Eph. 4:32; Col. 3:13).

The reason for this is clear: forgiving others enables us to receive the love and the power of God, and it also enables us to operate in the love and the power of God for the sake of others.

> '........................ (person's name), I release you right now from my anger and unforgiveness. I speak forgiveness over your life. I bless you in the name of Jesus and pray that the Lord will bless you too.'

For further reading

Mark Stibbe, *Prophetic Evangelism* (Authentic).

Session 10

The Practice of Prayer Ministry

Introduction

There are certain Dos and Don'ts. The important thing is to be filled with the Father's love and to give it away. Prayer ministry is the release of God's love to the wounded.

By offering prayer ministry, the local church shows that it cares for the spiritual, emotional and physical needs of every member of the body of Christ and, further afield, for the lost.

The following is a list of recommended guidelines for prayer ministry. Every one in the ministry team *must* respect these values and boundaries, otherwise people's dignity will be impaired:

1. Be prepared. Make sure there are tissues, dignity shawls, oil, tracts, follow-up cards, badges, mints, etc. Attend to your own dress sense and hygiene. Always be ready to minister.

2. Be watchful. Minister with your eyes open. Psalm 105:4 says, 'Keep your eyes open for God, watch for his works; be alert for signs of his presence' (The Message). If not, the person may:

- fall under the power of God
- manifest a demon
- walk away
- try to be aggressive, etc.

and you may miss the visible signs of the Spirit's power:

- flushes
- shaking
- eyelids fluttering
- tears, etc.

3. Be reliant. On the Holy Spirit, of course. Always invite the Spirit to be present for healing. Pray in the name of Jesus. 'I have seen your ministry, now it's time for you to see mine.'

4. Be discerning. What is the Father doing? He decides what needs to happen and how. Is this healing of the spirit, the soul or the body? What is God's will here? Use gifts of revelation:

- physical sensations
- pictures
- impressions
- words, etc.

5. Be wise. We do not pray for a person of the opposite sex on our own. Minister in pairs. Young people work alongside experienced people. We minister to kids with parental assent.

6. Be loving. Do to others what you would have others do to you. Help people to know they can trust you. Talk about God's love. Allay fears. Give people space. Be available to serve.

7. Be polite. Introduce yourself: 'Hello, I'm .... What's your name?' The question to ask then is, 'What is your need?' Or, 'What would you like the Lord Jesus to do for you?'

8. Be gentle. There is no need to push, to be rough, to speak unkindly, to shame, rebuke, etc. Aim to be like Jesus in everything. Stress confidentiality. Move the noisy!

9. Be patient. Wait for signs of the Holy Spirit's activity in the person's life. Allow the Lord space and time to do what he wants. Don't fill gaps with words. Work as a team.

10. Be sensible. Don't engage in directive prophetic statements, e.g. 'You will marry so and so.' Or, 'God says, "Throw away your medication."' Avoid manipulation and dependency on you.

11. Be biblical. Don't do or say anything that doesn't have a clear biblical basis. Give people Scriptures as well as pictures. Always have a Bible near to hand.

12. Be accountable. If out of depth, seek advice. If deliverance begins, inform the leader. If it's confession of sin, follow the guidelines in Session 9. Always report the following:

- when deliverance has clearly occurred
- when a person has come to the Lord
- when referral for pastoral prayer ministry is needed

- when a person wants to join a home group or Alpha course
- when an accident has happened
- when you have made a mistake

Conclusion

Remember, you do not engage in prayer ministry to have a visible profile or to have your own insecurities met. You do it in order to minister the Father's love to those in need.

Through the power of the Holy Spirit, and particularly with the help of the spiritual gifts, you are empowered to do the work of Jesus. You are a conduit of the healing presence of God to others.

It is absolutely vital that this kind of ministry takes place in an atmosphere of anointed worship and relational unity. Where the Spirit of the Lord is present (ungrieved), there is freedom.

How many of these guidelines are visible in the following story?

One day Peter and John were going up to the temple at the time of prayer – at three in the afternoon. Now a man crippled from birth was being carried to the temple gate called Beautiful, where he was put every day to beg from those going into the temple courts. When he saw Peter and John about to enter, he asked them for money. Peter looked straight at him, as did John. Then Peter said, 'Look at us!' So the man gave them his attention, expecting to get something from them. Then Peter said, 'Silver or gold I do not have, but what I have I give you. In the name of Jesus Christ of Nazareth, walk.' Taking him by the right hand, he helped him up, and instantly the man's feet and ankles became strong. He jumped to his feet and began to walk. Then he went with them into the temple courts, walking and jumping, and praising God (Acts 3:1–8, NIV).

- be prepared
- be watchful
- be reliant
- be discerning
- be wise
- be loving
- be polite
- be gentle
- be patient
- be sensible
- be biblical
- be accountable

Extra Notes

The Laying-On of Hands

Introduction

The Bible gives guidance for the laying-on of hands in the prayer ministry in the following contexts: blessing others, praying for others to receive the Holy Spirit, commissioning for ministry and healing.

1. PRAYING FOR PEOPLE TO BE BLESSED BY GOD

Hands are associated with praying in the Old Testament. The Jewish people to this day raise their hands to heaven as they pour out their prayers to God (Ps. 63:4, 77:2, 141:2). Just as we raise hands to heaven in prayer *to* God, so we lay hands on people in order to invoke a blessing *from* God. See Jacob's example (Gen. 48:14–16). NB Jesus continued this Jewish practice (Mk. 10.16; Lk. 24.50).

2. PRAYING FOR PEOPLE TO BE BAPTIZED IN THE SPIRIT

a. The Spirit may be given *without* the laying-on of hands.

- The Day of Pentecost (Acts 2:1–4)
- Cornelius' household (Acts 10:44–48)

b. The Spirit may be given *with* the laying-on of hands.

- The Samaritans (Acts 8:15–17; NB the imperfect tenses in v.17)
- The Conversion of Saul of Tarsus (Acts 9:17)
- The Ephesian Twelve (Acts 19:6)

Thus the Holy Spirit may be given to a person *through* the laying-on of hands (NB Acts 8:18 – *dia* in the original, meaning 'through').

The laying-on of hands is one way by which people receive the gift of the Spirit. Hands are often the human channel for the divine gift. This was the practice of the early church. Hands were laid on baptismal candidates and the following was prayed:

> O Lord God who has counted these thy servants worthy of deserving the forgiveness of sins and the laver of regeneration, make them worthy to be filled with the Holy Spirit (Hippolytus, second century).

Having said that, all God's people may do this, not just apostles or bishops (cf. Ananias in Acts 9). Those ministering to others through the laying-on of hands need to be, like Ananias, people of:

- Faith (Acts 9:10)
- Obedience (Acts 9:11)
- Devotion to God (Acts 22:12)

In other words, the channel must be pure.

3. PRAYING FOR PEOPLE TO BE COMMISSIONED IN MINISTRY

There are times when people set apart for a particular ministry are commissioned through the laying-on of hands. In this act there is a conferral of authority.

- Moses' prayer for Joshua (Num. 27:18, 20; Deut. 34:9)
- The seven deacons (Acts 6:1–6)
- Barnabas and Saul (Acts 13:3)
- Paul and Timothy (1 Tim. 4:14; 2 Tim. 1:6)

Clearly there is biblical precedent for the laying-on of hands in the context of commissioning, authorizing and dedicating people to a particular ministry, office or task in the church. This explains Paul's warning in 1 Timothy 5:22.

4. PRAYING FOR PEOPLE TO BE HEALED BY GOD

There are many occasions when those ministering in the healing gifts use the laying-on of hands. The following examples can be found in the New Testament:

- Jesus: Luke 4:40, Mark 6:5
- Paul: Acts 28:8
- Us: Mark 16:18

The one kind of healing ministry which never involves the laying-on of hands is deliverance. This, presumably, has to do with the danger of unclean spirits being transferred. We should avoid this practice when ministering deliverance.

Conclusion

The laying-on of hands is associated with a number of Spirit-inspired activities in the Scriptures. They are blessing, baptism in the Holy Spirit, commissioning and healing. I agree with Edward O'Connor:

> The gesture of laying on of hands does symbolize graphically the fact that God's grace is often mediated to a person through others, and especially through the community.

In recent decades we have rediscovered our hands in praying *to* God in worship (hands raised) and we have rediscovered our hands in asking for grace *from* God. The laying-on of hands is a biblical practice. But remember these rules:

- Be gentle
- Be decent
- Be sensible.

BIBLIOGRAPHY

St Augustine, *City of God*, Modern Library, 1994

Blue, Ken, *Authority to Heal*, IVP, 1987

Calvin, John, *Institutes of the Christian Religion*, Westminster John Knox Press, 1559 translation edition, 1960

Dunn, James, *Jesus and the Spirit*, Wm. B. Eerdmans Publishing Company, 1997

Edwards, Gene, *The Divine Romance*, Tyndale House Publishers, 1993

Eldredge, John, *Wild at Heart*, Thomas Nelson, 2001

John, J. & Stibbe, Mark, *The Big Picture 2*, Authentic, 2004

Kydd, Ronald, *Charismatic Gifts in the Early Church*, Hendrickson Publishers Inc., 1984

Kydd, Ronald, *Healing Through the Centuries*, Hendrickson Publishers Inc., 1998

MacNutt, Francis, *Healing*, Hodder & Stoughton Religious, 1997

Morphew, Derek, *Breakthrough: Discovering the Kingdom*, Struik Christian Books, 1991 (OP)

Stibbe, Mark, *Know Your Spiritual Gifts*, Zondervan, 1997

Stibbe, Mark, *Prophetic Evangelism*, Authentic, 2004

Wilson, Julian, *Wigglesworth: The Complete Story*, Authentic, 2002

Bibliography

Wimber, John, *Power Evangelism*, Hodder & Stoughton Religious, 1997

Wimber, John, *Power Healing*, Hodder & Stoughton Religious, 1986